# The Resonance of Unseen Things

# The Resonance of Unseen Things

POETICS, POWER, CAPTIVITY, AND

UFOS IN THE AMERICAN UNCANNY

Susan Lepselter

UNIVERSITY OF MICHIGAN PRESS

ANN ARBOR

Published in the United States of America by
the University of Michigan Press
Manufactured in the United States of America
⊚ Printed on acid-free paper

2019   2018   2017   2016      4   3   2   1

A CIP catalog record for this book is available from the British Library.

Library of Congress Cataloging-in-Publication Data

Names: Lepselter, Susan Claudia, author.
Title: The resonance of unseen things : poetics, power, captivity, and UFOs
    in the American uncanny / Susan Lepselter.
Description: Ann Arbor : University of Michigan Press, 2016. | Includes
    bibliographical references and index.
Identifiers: LCCN 2015043812| ISBN 9780472072941 (hardcover : alk.
    paper) | ISBN 9780472052943 (pbk. : alk. paper) | ISBN 9780472121540
    (ebook)
Subjects: LCSH: Human-alien encounters. | Conspiracy theories?United
    States.
Classification: LCC BF2050 .L47 2016 | DDC 001.942—dc23
LC record available at http://lccn.loc.gov/2015043812

# Acknowledgments

This book has morphed in and out of various emergent states for a very long time. It would be impossible to thank everyone who has deepened and expanded my thinking over the years—impossible both because I wish to keep confidential the names of multiple people to whom I am thankful for telling me their own stories, and also because so *many* people have influenced my ideas in ways too subtle and pervasive to describe. I offer my deepest gratitude to everyone who has talked with me about their own experiences, or shared with me any of the ideas that eventually took shape here. All weaknesses, omissions and errors in this book are my own.

For their generous support of this research, I sincerely thank the Wenner-Gren Foundation, the Rhonda L. Andrews Memorial Award, and the Andrew W. Mellon Foundation/Penn Humanities Forum. At the latter, I particularly thank Wendy Steiner for her support.

I thank the anonymous readers for University of Michigan Press for their knowledgeable and perceptive comments. Also at University of Michigan Press, I was very lucky to work with Aaron McCollough. I thank him for his keen sensitivity to language in his illuminating editorial improvements, for his balance of patience and persistence, and for his nimble support at a critical moment. I am grateful to Elizabeth Frazier at the Press, both for her very sharp eyes and for her equally impressive patience. Thanks as well to Christopher Dreyer, Allison Peters, and to Thomas Dwyer for support at an earlier stage.

I am deeply grateful to the professors whose teaching and scholarship early on modeled vivid ways to think about expressive culture. I am indescribably indebted to Katie Stewart for her intellectual example, support, and friendship over decades. Her luminous creativity as a thinker and writer of dazzlingly groundbreaking prose, and her singular capacity to evoke both the storied and unspoken elements of U.S. worlds have all been vital to me. I can't overstate the impact of Greg Urban's exuberant curiosity about the big questions of human culture and communication, and his rigorous attention to the smallest details of the same. Steven Feld taught his groundbreaking work on patterns of feeling and artfulness with simultaneous high theory and deep groove, along with his respect for and commitment to people, their art and their places. From my first encounters with Pauline Turner Strong, her anthropological perspective on the Indian captivity narrative and her innovative scholarship on this genre in America, was what first showed me that alien abduction was an iteration of this larger trope. I also deeply appreciate the input of time and energy, keen critical insight, and examples of brilliant scholarship by Robert Abzug, Ward Keeler, Ann Cvetkovich, and Joel Sherzer.

A few forums' focus on experimental, interdisciplinary work gave exceptional inspiration and provided meaningful critique for ideas in this book. I am grateful for the opportunity to have participated multiple times in Ethnographic Dreamworlds at Buffalo State College; I thank its creator, Allen Shelton, both for inviting me, and for his beautiful autoethnographic and theoretical writing. I am similarly grateful to have discussed versions of my ideas at the engaging "Mini AAAs" and other interdisciplinary venues made possible by the generosity and generativity of Michael Taussig. I am so grateful for the radical play of experimental writing and ideas that developed in the Writing/Worlding faculty working group at the University of Chicago. I thank Lauren Berlant both for organizing this critical/social experiment, and for sharing the invigorating flights of her own critical ideas in both talk and in writing. I am grateful to the helpful responses from members of the Bard College Lecture Series on Nature and Culture, organized by Laura Kunreuther. Also, I thank the Workshop on U.S. Locations and American Cultures at University of Chicago for inviting me to workshop a draft of what became the core of this book; the comments I received from the participants of the workshop were extremely helpful.

I give special thanks to Joe Masco. What began with a spontaneous group trip to Nevada has led to many years of generative conversation into the most unexpected, endlessly interesting aspects of the uncanny and the real in America; his brilliant scholarship continuously inspires me. I am especially grateful to Debbora Battaglia, whose extraordinary work and imagination continuously offers me new perspectives. I am indescribably grateful to both Joe and Debbora for their too-generous support and encouragement, in many ways, at crucial times. Input from Jodi Dean was pivotal at an important moment. Years ago, Robin Sheriff's insights into the sinister global dimension of alien abduction pushed my thinking in new directions. I thank Marilyn Ivy and John

Pemberton for entangling friendship and intellectual inspiration on the uncanny that encouraged the inception of this work many years ago.

Kathryn Lofton read the entire manuscript at an important moment and offered vital feedback. I am so grateful to her for her time, energy, and insight. I am also deeply grateful for rich and cogent feedback from Deborah Kapchan, Laura Kunreuther, Aaron Fox, Chris Roth, David Samuels, Louise Meintjes, Elana Zilberg, Erica David, Ben Feinberg, Calla Jacobson, Daniella Gandolfo, Deirdre de la Cruz, Susan Harding, Rosalind Morris, Yvette Christianse, David Valentine, Henry Goldschmidt, Ben Chesluk, and Heather Levi. I am so thankful for the support and rich intellectual stimulation of my colleagues and graduate students in my departments of American Studies and Communication and Culture, as well as in Folklore and Ethnomusicology and Anthropology, at Indiana University; here, I have received excellent editorial feedback from Ilana Gershon, Jane Goodman, Susan Seizer, Brenda Weber, Mary Gray, Sara Friedman, Michael Foster, Javier Leon, Diane Goldstein, Vivian Halloran, David Halloran, and Micol Seigel. Thanks as well to Aviva Goldstein, Claudia Heilbrunn, Alisa and Geoff Lepselter, Joan and Marty Lepselter, David Bleecker, Kate Neuman, Jenny Luray, Nancy Levene, Liz Rosdeitcher, Sandy Shapshay, and Karen Inouye for their support during this book's journey. Special thanks and appreciation to SALF.

There are many, many people who helped me on the ground in my research into stories, and while I do not have space to thank them all by name, I would like to express special gratitude to Bo, Hagar, Joe (G.), Rvanda, Elizabeth, Colin, Mary, Jeff, Dakota, Ellen, Monty, and Lisa, whose last names I omit in the interest of privacy. I owe enormous debts to Erma Jean Staffen and Stephen Miles Lewis, both of whose friendship, intellectual energy, and passion for big questions shaped my own thinking from the beginnings of my interest in this subject decades ago. Also in Texas, Audrey Meyer taught me, over years of inspiring friendship, about the power of prophecy and dreaming. In Nevada, people's incredible generosity and hospitality far exceeded my expectations. I am deeply grateful for the various ways that people helped me, took me to see their beautiful places, and shared their homes, their humor, and their stories. Again, it is impossible to name everyone. But I would like to express special gratitude to those who often took me into their homes or drove me around to see the land, especially Pat Travis and the late Joe Travis for their exceptional help;

Don Day; and Kaye and Jim Medlin for their generosity and Jim's time and skills as a guide. I am similarly thankful for the generous contributions of Jim and Mary Greenen, Jeanette Tholt, and to the late Arthur and La Rae Fletcher and Dolphina. I owe an enormous debt to the entire Nickell family for kindly showing me glorious parts of Nevada I would never have been able to know. I am also extremely grateful to help given by many other people both living and now passed on. Specifically I thank Carol Carter, Fay Day, Ann Morgan and Isaac Lopez, Dewayne Davis, Jack and Don Emery, Chuck Clark; the staff and regular patrons of the Little A'Le'Inn (especially Dee); and to the many other people who shared their stories with me. I have changed names, as well as many details, in these stories to protect privacy; nevertheless, I hope the feeling, rhythms, and themes still feel correct to the tellers.

# Contents

## CHAPTER I

# Vulnerabilities

This is not a book about UFOs. It's not a history of UFO belief, nor a sociology of believers. Rather, this is a book about a vernacular American poetics, something you can hear building up in the stories I will tell. The content of these stories varies, but their themes keep circling back to a sense that life in America is shaped by some ineffable, enormous power, a power that can be seen only in the patterns of its effects.

This book tracks both the form and the social life of the poetics I want to describe. I explore the prophetic desires and the historical iterations of its major trope, captivity. The stories here express public feelings and popular theories. And so this book is not about UFOs: rather, it follows the recursion and resonance between uncanny memories, hauntings, conspiracy theories, captivity narratives, and tales of everyday life.

Fantastic stories, like ordinary personal memories, arise amid experiences of class, loss, race, gender, and the body's unmoored location in a world of accelerated technological change. But those experiences aren't always articulated. Their shapes as stories are only partially visible from wherever one stands.

Many of the stories in this book were told to me directly, either one-on-one or in a group. Others are items of public culture: they come from grainy Xeroxed pages from UFO magazines, mass market popular books, academic theoretical books, radio, movies, newspapers and TV news, the Internet. The stories from all these media (from both academic and popular sources) are public signs that circulate through social space, and there are many ways that their intertextual flows can be tracked, critiqued, and analyzed. Through their connections, we can think about the interplay of public and intimate discursive domains. These stories let us follow that quick leg of the semiotic journey where the public sign is internalized, and then reproduced as another sign, or another story—one that's stained with other signs from the inner place it's been.

Some stories that I tell here came from hundreds of years ago, some from half a century ago, and some are from just the other day. Most of the stories I heard orally were told (or retold) at some point during a long stretch of the 1990s. When I think of that period now, it is like an eye in a hurricane. The First Gulf War was over, and the next wars against Iraq and Afghanistan had not yet begun. The World Trade Centers were standing, enormous and unmarked against the skyline. No one could yet have said that government bombs and not the planes caused the building to collapse, or that Flight 93 was completely staged, or that all the Jews and top financial traders stayed home that day. All the fraught events that quickly followed in the aftermath of the towers' destruction—the medicalized terror of anthrax scares, the secretive "code orange" days, the arguments for public safety through the erasure of civil liberties, and even years later, the growing uneasiness over the government's ability to read one's email or listen in on one's phone calls—all these still lay in the future. And yet for some people, when these anxious events did occur, they did not seem so very unfamiliar.

A sense of trauma fills many of the stories here. The referent of the trauma is elusive. The source is ambiguous not just for a skeptical critic but also as an element of the story itself. People telling these uncanny stories can only wonder about what really happened; but they just know *something is wrong.* Lauren Berlant has said that "the trauma produces something in the air without that thing having to be more concrete than a sense of the uncanny—free-floating anxiety in the room, negativity on the street, a scenario seeming to unfold within the ordinary without clear margins, even when a happening is also specific" (Berlant 2011: 80). This book explores the intense elaboration of this affect as it moves from a fleeting sensation into the center of things.

In the period when most of the ethnographic stories here arose, the Tea Party did not yet exist. Antigovernment conspiracy theory was commonly described in dominant media, if mentioned at all, as marginal or kooky. Before the mid-2000s, it was hard to imagine antigovernment conspiracy theorists achieving the empowered political base they found in the birther movement. Yet in many ways, libertarian discourses and movements based in a conspiratorial sensibility that achieved political ascendancy in the early twenty-first century were already latent, not just in the common populist strand long-standing in America, not in some quintessential "paranoid" quality of American character, but specifically in the uncanny talk that mushroomed in the 1990s.[1]

To remember a sense of the public sentiment of the beginnings of the time frame I'm going to explore here, you might think of it as the first year of the Clinton administration and ending, in 1999, as confusing predictions began to haunt the media with visions of an apocalyptic Y2K, when "the computers" would all break down and society would fall apart. My friends in rural Nevada were gearing up for Y2K with extra stores of canned food and ammunition; my friends in New York City laughed at how ridiculous the doomsday rhetoric in the media was, how technophobic, but filled their bathtubs with water on December 31, 1999. *You never know.*

In 1992, when I first met UFO believers in the midsize southern city I here call Hillview, *The X-Files* had not yet appeared on television.[2] There were still yellow ribbons hanging raggedly in some trees, leftovers from the Gulf War. In 1992, the country was in a recession. By 1998—when Hilary Clinton was mocked for accusing her husband's opponents of a "conspiracy"—there was an economic boom. But for many people, talk of booms and busts did not necessarily make a difference, except to the way they thought of themselves in relation to master narratives of class mobility. There was a sense that the true driving force of economic and political life in this country, and in the world, was not to be found in the surface ups and downs that might be declared on the news (see Dean 2009). Instead there was a sense of occult and sinister operations, something that went far beyond the moment's booms and busts and elections, back thousands of years, forward into the future, beyond America, beyond Europe, beyond the earth itself. There were forces of good and evil, forces that became manifest in our politicians but far transcended them. They gained power through their links to each other, building up strength and intensity through subterranean connections. There were things people did not name directly, but called these connecting forces *they* and *the powers that be.*

## Apophenia

Apophenia refers to the experience of perceiving connections between random or unrelated objects. This definition, though, already contains within it a specific point of view, an assumption of power. Who decides what is really related or unrelated? Who defines whether the relations between objects—or between events, or between spectacles of dominance across various contexts—are random and arbitrary?

In mainstream psychology, apophenia is called an "error of perception . . . the tendency to interpret random patterns as meaningful" (Hoopes 2011). But the people I write about here cultivate apophenia, not as an "error," but instead as a way to begin seeing those things that have become invisible. They foreground the naturalized patterns that normally go without saying. It is in one sense an endless bricolage (Lévi-Strauss 1966), but rather than building something concrete from the "odds and ends" at hand, here the product is never finished; you select the part for the rush of its echo to another part. Here each found or revealed sign leads on to other resemblances, other openings.

The people here pay close attention to parallels and resemblances between stories. And the parallels produce a feeling of, and an aesthetic sense of, resonance.[3] And, I argue, the resonance itself becomes another story. The sense of uncanny resonance becomes an expressive modality, a vernacular theory, a way of seeing the world, an intimation of the way *it all makes sense.* It becomes both performance and theory, creating a sense of an occult design that might someday be apprehended below the jumbled surfaces of the ordinary. Accumulating and recursive images, and the felt connections between them, reveal how historical trauma gets lodged in the bright, broken bits of fantastic things.

I use the term "resonance" in this book to mean the intensification produced by the overlapping, back and forth call of signs from various discourses. The uncanny narratives here acquire affect, intensity, and meaning through their resonance and dissonance with other more familiar cultural narratives, those that can seem like the inevitable shape of the real and are less overtly marked as constructed narratives. Resonance describes the social, affective, and aesthetic dimension of a perspective based in apophenia, finding connections between signs, and often understanding that process as political. Here those connections are based on resemblance and repetition. This effect entails mimesis, but the resemblance is partial and fluid. It is *felt.* And the intertextual connections feel vertically layered, rather than horizontally bridged.

Resonance is not an exact reiteration. Rather it's something that strikes a chord, that inexplicably rings true, a sound whose notes are prolonged. It is just-glimpsed connections and hidden structures that are felt to shimmer below the surface of things. It is what makes people say, *It all fits together* and *Something just clicked* and *My whole life I just felt like something was going on, and this explains it.* And as I describe later, that sense of resonance gives rise to the partial sense of familiarity that makes an experience classically uncanny, where the strange leads back to what you already knew.

## Abductions

People I met in Hillview, and at UFO conferences in the Southwest, often told the same origin story about how their lives shifted into a register that included extensive thinking and talking about aliens; the story was about discovering Whitley Strieber's book *Communion: A True Story.* They said just *seeing* the book changed their lives. Strieber was already a successful writer of gothic fantasy fiction when he described his own weird alien abduction experiences in *Communion.* People said they'd been browsing in a bookstore and suddenly came upon *Communion* displayed on a table. They were flooded with feelings and half-memories; they got a palpable shock, and they knew then *this is what happened to me.* Even before they identified with Strieber's strange narrative and its tone of anguished questing, the visual cover image struck people with the immediacy and intensity of revelation. It was the first time they saw a picture of that iconic alien face dominated by enormous black eyes like a giant insect, or like a Nazi in a gas mask, or a surgeon peering down at you as you veered in and out of awareness on the table. But also like none of those things exactly, not specifically one of them alone. People I met said it was that cover—and then the book—that made them *remember things* they had already known and, over time, forgotten.

Throughout that decade, alien abduction discourse mushroomed. People passed around battered paperbacks by Budd Hopkins telling abduction stories from his work with abductees. Hopkins's books widely circulated the now-familiar abduction narrative: how aliens come to your bedside, paralyze you, silence you, and float you out of the room and into their nightmarish surgeries. His colleagues in abduction research added to the picture common hallmarks of captivity: how "abductees commonly feel that data of some sort is being extracted from their minds" (Jacob 1992: 97).[4] How they steal not just thoughts and feelings but your eggs and sperm, the babies in your womb. How the aliens put trackers up your nose, silently follow you year after year so you can just feel that presence. And how they do this while all the time calming you, pacifying you, making it impossible to break free.

The image, the idea, the word, the story, struck a chord: *abduction* seemed instinctively, uncannily real. People felt an organizing convergence of a vaguely ominous sense. The word itself, *abducted*, with its Latinate sound and hard split as your lip pops between its consonants, was somehow more clinical and official than "kidnapped," the *duct* inside it a rushing force, a channel that carries you away. *Abduction* expressed an overspilling sensation of captivity and containment by something you can't control, communicated a feeling about the unseen forces that inscribed your body and tracked your movements, controlled your memory, and did things to your reproductive organs . . . it *just made sense*, it just fit in with the feeling people said they'd already been having. Some people acted on this feeling and underwent hypnosis with therapists sympathetic to the abduction experience, to see if they might unearth a whole memory. Many people have, through hypnosis, recalled alien abduction. Many others remain in the liminal space where the haunting feeling of abduction brings together a nagging, familiar sense of *a something* that was already there.

You could say all that in different words, a new vocabulary—perhaps, now, in words that make that same kind of intuitive sense to *me*. Another way of describing an image or idea that seems to organize a whole range of feelings and social experiences, that appears in stories of different kinds and links them together, that makes a pattern out of things you never before knew how to pull together, is to see it as a trope. The more I heard over the years about things *just fitting together*, the more it seemed clear that abduction itself was a greatly capacious trope, one that was changeable and alive. But abduction was only half the trope. The other half of abduction was release, the coming through containment to the other side.

There are so many facets to this trope, piling up into an enormous set of resonating images that might never be an entire whole. I locate the trope throughout this book in a different ways. It appears in various forms, and it is shot through with shifting sentiments in different contexts.

There is abduction and release; there is captivity and restoration. There is paralysis, and there is mobility. There is the centripetal force of containment, and there is the centrifugal force of flight (Bakhtin 1981). There is the captivity of amnesia and the release of recollection. All these are connected expressions of a larger structure, a broad figure that includes all of these dimensions of captivity and liberation. And it is grounded in the forceful insistence of *freedom* as a master metatrope of American national identity, and a way of storying what you might say *this way* if you were an academic historian: that "the glorification of freedom [is] the essential characteristic of American life in a struggle for global dominance" (Foner 2003).

In 1994, the Harvard psychiatrist John Mack wrote *Abduction*, describing his psychological work with UFO abductees. Because of Mack's academic and writerly credentials (he had previously won a Pulitzer for a biography of Lawrence of Arabia) *Abduction* generated a wider attention than UFO books usually did. Mack said the way truth was figured by official, elite perspectives was out of touch with truth on the ground, where a new paradigm was taking shape, an ability to transcend the binary of material and imagined realms. Other prominent alien abduction researchers whom the people I knew talked about (for example, Budd Hopkins and David Jacobs) had insisted that alien abduction was by definition sinister and violating. If abductees had a positive experience, either they hadn't really been abducted—they were "confabulating" (Jacobs 1992)—or their experience offered more evidence that aliens pacified their victims through deceit. But Mack veered into spiritual and New Age ideas; alien abduction led to transformation, for "unlike human abusers" and political kidnappers, these "beings reveal a shared purpose, and offer the possibility of openings to inclusive more expansive worldview" (Mack 1994: 399).[5] Still, Mack authored a report with Hopkins and Jacobs, based on a Roper Poll of "personal experiences" the three had sponsored. As Jacobs wrote, "The results of the Roper Poll indicated that millions of Americans might be abductees . . . the final analysis indicates that 2 percent of the American people—five million Americans—have experienced events consistent with those that abductees experienced before they knew they were abductees" (Jacobs 1998: 123). Many people reported that they had, for example, wakened paralyzed with a strange figure in the room, seen a terrifying figure, left their bodies, had missing time, seen a ghost, flown through the air, had puzzling scars. They came from "almost all groups in society" (124). The signs of abduction were everywhere.

Carla and I were friends from the Hillview UFO experiencers' group. She and I watched John Mack on TV one evening, on *48 Hours*. He had a serious, soulful face, spoke of his patients in intelligent and respectful tones. When I spoke with Mack once, in the 1990s, he thoughtfully said that psychiatrists must listen to their patients from a stance of belief.

And the abductees who appeared with Mack on TV were professional people; they were believable and sane, speaking not just of violation but of that *something more*—the transformation, the redemption or release. Some had made it to the other side. We sat in Carla's little house, with her paperbacks piled everywhere, books on ancient UFOs and spirit religions and political conspiracies and psychology. She smoked pensively, petting her dog, and acknowledged that Mack—even though he was appearing on suspiciously mainstream TV—*was pretty good.* Mack was respectful of his patients, his book told their stories faithfully, he marveled at the similarities between their memories and did not explain anything away. Carla approved of his "new perspectives," and she too believed that alien abduction was part of a wider spiritual growth. She liked how he said the people weren't crazy. Carla sometimes said that only people who *had gone through things* in childhood were open enough to be chosen, to be abducted or taken up and out of the banal realm of everyday life. The wounds of life left you primed for a *something more* than this shit down here. But she still talked about the gray aliens in clinical registers, and the sinister abduction horror story still dominated popular narrative.

## Explosions

Through the 1990s, the image of the alien kept exploding in popular culture; talk of UFOs and representations of extraterrestrials were everywhere (see Dean 1998; Brown 2007; Badmington 2004). This wave of 1990s alien images was cheerfully popping up in everything from new television shows (like *The X-Files*) to movies (like *Fire in the Sky* in 1993, the Hollywood rendition of a UFO abduction testimony whose book version had been important to believers for years).[6] In the 1990s, suddenly, everywhere you looked there were inscrutable bumper stickers featuring black alien head icons, a series of images mysteriously called "Schwa" stickers after the company that made them.[7] Alien images became part of a hipster 1990s aesthetic—a kind of "alien chic" (Badmington 2004) that signaled what Badmington (2004) has described as a posthumanist embrace of the other within, a refusal to maintain the rigid us/them boundaries that had marked warlike aliens at the height of the Cold War. On one level these 1990s "chic" alien images performed a rejection of the older us/them national identity. But the social worlds where people felt passionate about the meaning of UFOs were not chic at all. People who organized their lives around UFO belief knew that talking about them urgently and earnestly was still generally a stigmatized and trivialized practice. It was still linked to "the tabloids" as a code for the debased habitus of an imaginary group of uneducated, lower-class Americans (Dean 2009, 1998).

Some people's intellectual and social lives revolve around the quest to reduce the stigma of UFO belief; as they put it, they want UFO investigations to "go mainstream." But there are other people who passionately organize their lives around UFOs in a way that expressively embraces and identifies with their marginality. The rapidly proliferating signs of UFOs in the public domain, in TV shows and movies and books, didn't sit well with those who felt intuitively that UFOs belonged to the unincorporated realm of *the weird stuff*. They didn't want UFO belief to "go mainstream." And they didn't trust "Science" to approach the mystery of UFOs without killing something irreducible in what that mystery meant to them. For these people, the fact that most folks *just didn't get it* was the point.

I met some of these people in the Hillview UFO Experiencers Support Group. I was led to the Experiencers through a local chapter of its parent group, the Mutual UFO Network (MUFON). MUFON is an international organization whose mission is to make UFOs a credible topic of scientific investigation and Hillview has an active chapter. There were some intellectual and strategic differences between the two local groups in Hillview (though people often participated in both), but the Experiencers Support Group was my primary ethnographic home base in the overlapping Hillview UFO worlds. I did fieldwork in these groups, though primarily in the support group, for a total of two years, maintaining friendships with a few members for many years afterward.

Many people in these overlapping communities arranged their political, social, and emotional affinities not around ideas of a "left" or a "right" political wing but always around ideas of invisible centers of power (cf. Dean 2009). In this specific structure of feeling and imagination, the margins oppose that occult, sinister center, a black hole that invisibly sucks people into its gravitational pull. My closest friend in the UFO support group eventually drifted into a social world that actively sympathized with the militia movement. It was sometimes difficult to understand her support for right-wing militias along with her intense championship of gay rights and gender nonconformity. Many UFO believers plucked stances from both traditional right- and left-wing ideologies, relating not to traditional activist political lines but instead to a sense of distance from the *powers that be* (see Dean 2009, 1998). The "prepper" bookstore I visited in Nevada displayed militia manifestos and apocalypse-preparedness handbooks next to Noam Chomsky's *Manufacturing Consent.*

Carla could smell appropriation and incorporation from miles away. She hated the way *the UFO thing is everywhere now.* For Carla, talking about UFOs expressed her distance from a sinister power that tried to control ordinary people. The power came in various manifestations, emerging in bloody centuries of the past and secret cabinets in Washington today. As *the powers that be*, it was always present in some form. If you weren't careful, it incorporated you into its zombified center where you could no longer think for yourself. After a while, Carla left the UFO Experiencers group and joined another group that fervently studied the Constitution as a redemptive, sacred democratic text.

Carla had politicized her distance from *the powers that be* in a way that would soon itself become mainstream in populist public culture, forcing her to move on yet again. After a while she was no longer talking so fervently about UFOs, inner dimensions, or unusual spiritual experiences, but more and more about the New World Order, the threat of worldwide socialism, and the plots that global networks were secretly planning with then-attorney general Janet Reno, the Trilateral Commission, and wealthy powers that be across the brutalized body of the world.

After a few more years, her constitutional study group itself could not express what she was looking for in the peripheries. She and her new intellectual companions saw that the world as they knew it was ending.

Many people do end their worlds, unworlding what they've made (Stewart 2007), drifting off to spin a new one. After Carla left, the little UFO Experiencers group passed into the hands of a bright, intense, self-educated young man named "Lenny," with a keenly organized, passionate take on every bit of literature he had ever seen on the topic of the paranormal. He started a zine, created one of the first solid online presences I knew of, read and discussed everything from physics to psychedelic speculation. Carla and I continued to call and email each other for years, talking about what was going on in the world as she saw it, until our friendship drifted too.

Later on, I participated in another community of uncanny storytellers in central Nevada, a land of both drifters and homesteaders. Rachel, Nevada, is a rural hamlet located on the border of the vast military-industrial complex of Nellis Air Force Bombing and Gunnery Range and the Nevada Test Site, and the secret military base called Groom Lake, or Area 51. Although the U.S. government finally admitted its existence in 2013, Area 51 then was literally an enormous open secret: four million acres of unacknowledged bomb range (Patton 1998; Jacobsen 2011). Its 4,742 miles of restricted airspace (Patton 1998: 3) are known as Dreamland. And in fact the secret was a dream of the Cold War come to life in the desert, a hugely funded, technological project of the Atomic Energy Commission, the Department of Energy, and the U.S. military in conjunction with private contractors like Wackenhut and Lockheed. This is the place that produced covert aircraft like the stealth bomber and the U2, the place that supposedly built the fabled Mach 6 speed plane *Aurora*. The base is connected to the Nevada Test Site and the nuclear detonations that occurred for decades there. Local people in the area still talk about seeing the buildings set up around the test site, and then seeing their ruins (see Masco 2006). Here, amid lingering Cold War secrets and the continuing development of war machines, aliens perhaps inevitably came to live like the "Martian in the Machine" described by Jackie Orr: "A new fear encased in an old story of monsters wielding magical, murderous weapons? Or an old fear encased in a new frequency, exciting strange electronic fields of as-yet-uncharted human motion?" (Orr 2005: 40).

I made my first visit to Rachel in 1997 because of the UFO stories I'd heard about this place from people in Hillview. (I do not use a false name for the town of Rachel, as I do for Hillview, because Rachel is already public, a well-known destination for UFO tourism.) There were indeed plenty of similar tales floating around in Rachel. But once there, what I more vividly heard was the restless interplay between uncanny and ordinary stories. This was a place not just for "conspiracy theorists" but also for hardworking western people with strong community bonds, valuing the decency of everyday accomplishments and a fierce attachment to a legacy of independence. The inextricability of the uncanny and the ordinary expressed a particular blend of desire and nostalgia—a mix of otherworldly displacement and the deep specificity of a heavily entextualized, lived-in place in the American West. The ways these discourses came together suggested other kinds of anxiety about colonization and the earth, secrecy and theft, nature and loss, and the vulnerable boundaries of the human body. These were themes—about strange, amorphous power and the vulnerability of unsuspecting subjects—I'd also heard in the UFO groups in Hillview.

The central meeting point in Rachel is a UFO-themed café called the Little A'Le'Inn. After my first brief visit there, I called the owners to ask if I could waitress that fall at the Little A'Le'Inn, to write about the stories I heard. Someone had just quit, and Pat said I could live with her and Joe, in their mobile home next to the café, in lieu of waitress wages. I waitressed there again the following summer, this time living again with Pat, Joe, and another waitress for part of the time, and partly in a separate mobile home with my husband, when he came with me to Nevada for a month.

Joe, who owned the café with his wife Pat, believed in many of the same things as Carla. Both Joe and Carla were charismatic storytellers with abandoned origins in charismatic churches. And they were both driven by the partial designs they saw—architectures of conspiracy, webs of the *powers that be* whose hidden strands you could tease out, a bit at a time, through talk. Like the other people I write about here, their sense of hidden meaning was an "occult cosmology," the term used by Sanders and West to describe the "ontological dimensions" of covert systems (Sanders and West 2003: 6).

Like Carla, Joe had always just felt it in his bones: *Something was wrong.* And one day for him too, he said, *It all clicked*, it *all came together*, everything *just made sense* as a plot by the powers that be. But Joe, who had a poor childhood, was now making a good living at his café. Though he liked to keep life simple, he owned his mobile home, and he'd bought land. By midlife he was in a stable, long-term third marriage. Carla was moving around, still trying to find the right place.

She had nothing fixed in place but her convictions, her fierce intellect, and her ability to meet new people who, for a while, formed a world with her, based on a feeling that there was always a *something more.*

## Vulnerabilities

For some people the ominous powers in the world came into sharpest relief as a coherent belief when the Bureau of Alcohol, Tobacco, Firearms and Explosives raided David Koresh's Branch Davidian compound in Waco, Texas in 1993 (see Fenster 2008). The Waco incident crystallized an already-developed sense of *how things are* and played out this sense of subterranean sinister developments in an overt, concrete display of government violence against civilians. There it was, on the news: the government was killing people who didn't toe the line. *They* could come and do it to anyone who wanted to live the way they saw fit. The media was *part of it,* showing things in the news from only their own side: they were the ones who demonized Koresh and let the government off the hook, keeping the public in its perpetual state of deception. It was maybe even worse than Ruby Ridge the year before: now it seemed *they* were going after not just overt independence and freedom but also spiritual belief.

The day of the fire in Waco, Carla called me in sorrow and outrage. I had been watching the TV news about Koresh stockpiling weapons; I was too stunned by the whole disaster to make any immediate judgment (although soon afterward I came to agree with Carla about the criminality of the raid there). *What do you think!* she asked, in a slow voice of controlled anger, testing me, testing my position on an invisible line. I did not yet know what I thought. She heard the newscaster brand the Branch Davidians a "cult." She said:

What is a cult?
A cult is a culture.
A cult is a culture
That they don't like.

she said.
And she added,

*We are supposed to have religious freedom in this country . . .*
*It's all a lie.*

For Carla, watching the Waco complex burn was at once a terrible revelation and a confirmation of what she already just knew in her bones: that unseen powers, consortiums of the media, the government, and covert groups of the rich, elite, and powerful, were intentionally testing the American people. They used a rumor of David Koresh's crimes of sexual abuse to play on easy American sentiment, she said. The Waco compound was a lethal *experiment* they conducted on ordinary people, *to see what they could get away with.* And, she noted, they did get away with it. No one watching the news revolted. To Carla, and to many other people who thought like her, the Branch Davidian fire was a declaration of war by the powers that be.

There is much to say about the ways that such incidents, especially the raids upon Ruby Ridge in 1992 and Waco (and to some extent before that, the bombing of MOVE in 1986 Philadelphia) helped catalyze militia movements and talk of the New World Order in the United States (see Fenster 2008; Barkun 2003; Sanders and West 2006). But here I want to focus on Carla's way of speaking, as a way in to what she saw in the discourse about Waco.

She said: *A cult is a culture!*—and this was a kind of poetic register that best expressed the truth. For Carla (and for many of her intellectual and political companions) it was vital to avoid being duped by the TV anchor's authoritatively referential register, which he used to intone Koresh's evil. Listening with her point of view in mind, you can hear it with ears tuned to the pervasive performance of power. The voice of the news broadcaster was a monologic appropriation, a performance that justified *their* actions by claiming the singular point of view (cf. Bakhtin 1981). This referential-based register—the performance style of the powers that be—denied the hidden, piled-up connections between things, to paint a lulling picture of rational cause and effect. But perhaps you could discover the deep structure of things in verbal parallelism and hints of hidden relationships. *They* rationalized their violence by calling Koresh's group "a cult," defining it in a totalizing move. But attending to the verbal resemblance between *cult* and *culture* gave Carla the insight that what *they* called a "cult" was in fact a coherent entity of meanings and traditions, which is what she thought of as "a culture." The Koresh compound was an autonomous culture that deserved its own sovereignty—*but one that they don't like.* Noticing the parallel between the words cult and culture allowed her a swift insight into the validity of difference and outrage at its oppression in this case.

Just as there are overlaps between various sources of power, then—between the media and the government and other hidden groups—there are resonating overlaps in words. You could just glimpse a grammar of the real here, through iconicities of language. *Culture* containing *cult* pointed to a larger etymology of things beyond language itself, a structure glinting through the words that represented it. Cult and culture clicked. For Carla there was always a sense of the inextricable poetic and political hidden structure in the world, between many different things. There really was no separating the poetic and the political. And that sensibility is what I want to explore as I tell stories throughout this book.

## Working with the Real

But the unavoidable question—*Are UFOs real?*—haunts research on UFO belief in a way that would be inconceivable with, for instance, ethnographic research on spirit possession. What about the physical traces left by UFOs, the unexplained scars on the bodies of abductees, the multiple viewings? Doesn't this, one might ask, point to their reality?

The question of the real has brought alien abduction stories into other forms of memory research. In the late 1990s and into the twenty-first century, a team of Harvard psychologists were studying memory in people who had (after periods of forgetting) recovered memories of sexual abuse. But a control group was needed, people whose memories of traumatic events, they dryly wrote, "are unlikely to have occurred" (Clancy et al. 2002). For this control group, they decided on alien abductees. In 2002, they published a paper in the *Journal of Abnormal Psychology*, concluding that alien abductees, although not mentally ill in any way, were more prone to false recall and recognition than people without false memories. In the course of their work, the team concluded that people who remember being abducted by aliens were really suffering from sleep paralysis in the liminal state between sleeping and waking. The sleep-paralysis explained the stories of immobility, powerlessness, and being taken over. The rest of it was the influence of movies and TV shows.

For students of folklore, the theory of sleep paralysis as the biological basis of some uncanny visitation experiences is not a new idea. Decades before, for example, David Hufford investigated stories and memories of "hagging" in Newfoundland, an event in which the supernatural "old hag" sits on the victim's chest in the night, paralyzing and immobilizing them, leaving people with a sense of mute suffocation and terror (Hufford 1982). In what he called an "experience-centered" theory of supernatural attacks, Hufford connected many world traditions that seem to narrate similar phenomenologies. Twenty years before the Harvard study, Hufford theorized that sleep paralysis is a universal occurrence that may underlie many traditions of traumatic uncanny attack. However, rather than dismiss the uncanny memories, his respectful and careful study emphasized the primacy of human embodied experience, as a way to insist on the phenomenological reality of stories that might easily be seen as folklore in the sense of fiction.[8]

Hufford's nuanced sense of the real in the experience of uncanny

trauma is not necessarily easily achieved. In *Abducted* (the book intro-
ducing the sleep paralysis abduction theory to a more popular audience
than readers of *Journal of Abnormal Psychology*), Susan Clancy (one of
the authors of the original Harvard study and a graduate student at the
time it was conducted) recounts how she listens to her subjects' abduction memories and then their incredulity when she tries to tell them
they were merely experiencing sleep paralysis. Why, she wonders in
the book, won't they listen to reason?

But not all abduction reports are the same, any more than are all
memories of sexual abuse. Not all abduction memories take place in bed
while the person's falling asleep, or while being woken from sleep by
aliens. Even among people who do start their stories in the liminal state
surrounding sleep, there can be idiosyncratic details that are not easily
dismissed as being "copied" from a recent television show. At the same
time, they may well reveal both biological and phenomenological experience, and social as well as individual meaning. In other words, in order
to yield significant meaning, memories of uncanny trauma do not necessarily have to be reduced to a question of whether the abduction "really
happened"—something impossible to assess after the fact in any case.

For me, *the real* presents other questions. What happens when you
listen to UFO talk ethnographically—when the uncanny is shot
through with the ordinary noise of life? Then you hear many kinds of
stories, and silences, all filled with multiple, layered senses of being
abducted or caught, and multiple dreams of release. These are stories
filled with interconnecting imaginaries of injury and redemption.
Some memories are branded clearly into narrativized awareness. Other
memories are more like backgrounds or shadows that give depth and
emotional weight to things visible on the surface.

How do you let yourself know, in the theories and stories you are
told, the weight of the past or the intimations of the future, and to take
them seriously as signs (and signs of what)? How do you direct the will
toward that referent long enough "to follow ghosts . . . to follow where
they lead, in the present, head turned backwards and forwards at the
same time" (Gordon 1997: 57)? It requires attention to the story itself;
to "be willing to follow ghosts" as they appear in narrative is to follow
the shades of the story. It's to place your step inside its prints and
"track along in its wake" (Stewart 1996) so that "the real" has a chance
to crystallize not as an outside referent, but inside the story itself.

To be clear: I am not a UFOlogist, and I do not know more than
anyone else about the physical reality of UFOs. What I do look at here

is how the question of the real is constantly deconstructed in the discourse itself. People talk about a space that slides between "memory" and "dream," subverting the discrete borders of the real. This is a book about stories and discourses—traces of loss and accelerative bits of imagination, in real, material utterances, agitations of the air.

And so the stories here are the real objects. They are performative, a form of verbal art. Attention to their formal properties entails a kind of ethnopoetics—not in the usual sense of analyzing the poetics of a non-Western culture, but rather those of a strange mirror, reflecting and distorting the dominant discourses imploding inside an empire.

Although this book depends on people who shared their talk with me over the course of many years, it is not an ethnography in the traditional sense, and the object of my study does not emerge in a single, unified place. For decades, many contemporary ethnographers have been developing more contingent and multiple objects of study. The senses of place that are deeply, ambivalently felt in people's lives and various other places are, to be sure, components of the themes I want to explore. But this book is about neither a unified, emplaced American subculture nor a clearly marked-off genre. Therefore, the structure of the book mimetically performs the multiple, fragmentary, but parallelistic nature of the sometimes elusive object I want to track.

Throughout, I try to suggest how through story, the sinister, the traumatic, and the disintegrated can recuperate sociability and meaning. To try to relay this impression, at times I present objective bits of discourse. These clearly bounded stories are marked as formal narratives, either through emphasis of their poetic form, or by use of quotations. At other times, my voice opens up to a play of reported speech, in a kind of ethnographic version of poetic ventriloquism (S. Stewart 1995) or a form of "contaminated critique" (K. Stewart 1991).[9] At times, in the critical mode developed by scholars such as Kathleen Stewart (1996, 2007), I try to represent other people's verbal style inside my own voice, presenting their words as reported speech inside a story I myself am telling—erasing neither of us, but opening up my memory and interpretation to their words, and compressing us both into the imaginative and hermeneutic zone that, through my writing, we share. I often let the narratives themselves perform their own analysis; as Feld puts it, "Stories create analytic gestures . . . [and] stitching together stories is a sense-making activity," both for me as a listener, and for the people about whom I write (Feld 2012: 8).[10]

Therefore, this book sometimes performs the way uncanny stories grow powerful: through the sense of truth that accumulates out of a cultivated apophenia and its built-up, intertextual parallelism. The voices here slip between abstract theory and concrete image. I am trying to show that the stories themselves *are* theories, dramatic voicings of epistemological positions. And so my own style of representation moves between a performative mimesis of other people's voices, and more clearly bounded "theoretical" or "ethnographic" observations, as I try to saturate you here in the dense poetics that have saturated me. I want my "hybridized" voice to convey the powerful force of stories that might be too easily dismissed or rationalized by a more distanced kind of analysis. I want to suggest how seductive this narrative force is when you encounter it—how good it is at spinning a discursive field that supports its own logics, and how well it can permeate the resistance of other systems.

I do not use my own theoretical voice to clearly stand above the others, easily explaining or forgiving their excesses and illogics, because that is not consistent with my experience of this discourse. Rather my experience of listening was of being narratively and poetically infected, altered—not as a full-fledged conversion, but as a destabilizing opening into other kinds of theories and other structures of imagination. My style here therefore performs the ethnographic experience of hybridization and partial permeation, as a way of dealing with the very real, often disturbing, seductive power of the discourses I present, and with their prolific growth in America.

Therefore, my multiple focuses on American imaginaries do not remain inside the boundaries of any unified culture or place. Rather, I follow the intertextual nature of social and poetic processes, in genres of uncanny memory, fantastic prophecy, and accounts of everyday life common to my interlocutors. As Debbora Battaglia has put it, "Theirs is a fluid sociality of contact consciousness in an alien key" (Battaglia 2005: 3).

The object here is still something that I observed and helped people to make. But the "thing" that people make, here, is not one single story, myth, or poem form. Instead the "thing" they make is the intertextual, poetic process of recognizing the resemblances and patterns of other stories, and using that chime to cast a new story. The impact of these chimes, the strange half-rhyme people here feel down to their feet, sometimes arises from the hidden, the unspoken, and the forgotten. It is a quality of apophenia, the making of connections from felt pasts and future intimations.

## Resonant Apophenia

Questions remain, however. What was abducted from a person, and who was doing it? What in the experience of power fit so well with stories of uncanny abducting forces? What is the inarticulate and half-forgotten material that adds the resonant urgency and feeling of depth to stories of alien abduction and uncanny conspiracy?

Though it is never a one-to-one kind of symbol, the accumulated stories that point to a forgotten *something* do suggest what that something might be. There are stories of class and its invisible, unmarked limitations, and stories of race and gender, and the small, multiple ways that a life is disappointed by master narratives of progress and success. There are stories of nuclear fear, resonating in scattered and displaced effects within everyday life, the "psychic effect" that Masco (2006) has illuminated as the "nuclear uncanny."[11] There are stories of the federal government's mid-twentieth-century experiments on poor people: giving children plutonium-laced cereal, feeding them radioactive snacks after luring them to join the Science Club at school, and giving pregnant hospitalized women plutonium in what were said to be vitamins (Welsome 1999). There are images of the body's containment in what feel like strange new medical developments, cloning, surrogate pregnancies of poor women for rich women. There are images here that echo the medical experiments done in Nazi concentration camps. There are images of slaves in America, of the middle passage in a strange ship going to a strange new world. There are images of centuries of colonial genocide of Native American people, in a quick afterimage that flashes in the cowboy and Indian movie that you went to as a white kid decades ago, when for a second you rooted for the wrong side, and didn't register anything except a feeling of *something wrong* . . . Linked up with the variable infinite experience of class, race, gender and loss, it is the *parallels* between these stories about power that *become the subject* of many uncanny stories. The original stories of historical trauma don't always make it up for air. (If they did, they would no longer haunt.)

Instead, the uncanny story itself is about the resemblances between the unspoken originals. The urge toward apophenia begins to resonate and hum. And that resonance is something to notice too, because it is a story of power on its own. And that, in fact, is the object of this book.

CHAPTER 2

# Secret Immobilities and the Poetics of the Uncanny

I begin with a few assumptions.

First, I assume that stories contain their own form of theory.

Second, I assume that I know more when I draw on different realms of discourse, from the clearly marked theories of multiple academic disciplines, to the implicit theory that is always inside a vernacular story.

Third, I assume that my own voice in writing is always an open and mimetic instrument. While some of my prose will follow academic theoretical and analytic conventions, other parts will follow narrative conventions that I hear in ethnographic contexts.

This book swings between stories and theories to illustrate my understanding of the social and poetic life of the uncanny. It's shot through, at each point, with the unspoken, infinitely varied containments of power and class, desire, and a sense of something missing.

## Missing Limb

Some guys were working on our house in Hillview,[1] and Junior, the handyman with a missing leg, was going progressively insane. It took me days to notice that anything might be amiss, because it seemed everyone was talking about things from other worlds. Junior's smart, pragmatic partner Eddy came into the kitchen for a drink of water; he talked about his dreams of going underground, about storing what you need *down there* to survive when this government shit hits the fan. Eddy said he's planning to buy *invisible land.* It was chitchat while he drank instant iced tea at the table.

But Junior was really unraveling. He'd seen the saucers in the desert himself; he'd seen them spin into underground bases. He implied unspeakable dangers. At the kitchen table, he drew diagrams, charts and graphs, and quick loops and loops of the spinning. But to some extent these were the same stories and the same kinds of drawings I knew from ordinary, very sane people who were into UFOs—city employees who entered data in clean white offices, busy mothers, short-order cooks, secretaries, and tech workers. These were people who had no mental illness. The UPS man, hearing about my interests, stood on the porch and described seeing a UFO as a kid. *Man it just took off, just like that.* Talking about this was part of a discursive world, and it did not mean one lived outside the ordinary boundaries of quotidian, practical life.

But then Junior said *they* stole his leg because he knew too much. *It's a warning.* Next, he said, *they* would take his life. He became aware of sinister electronic codes. These were tones that would kill whoever heard the right combination. He beeped the lethal sequences into his phone and pager, thinking he could kill the sinister listener on the other end by remote control. We could overhear the poor guy Junior had called, yelling hello? hello? to the sound of the pushbutton beeps, and when the beeps didn't kill the guy, Junior grumbled, saying, *Jeez nothing works anymore.*

My housemate and I hastily drove Junior to his brother's house across town. It was his only family. We explained to the sister-in-law what had happened and advised her to get Junior some help. We thought we'd done what we could for Junior, telling his family about his spiraling down, figuring they'd find a way to save him. But a couple of days later he stolidly walked the five miles back to our house, in the hot southern sun, on his one leg. The stump was bloody and sore over the prosthetic. There was obviously nowhere left for him to go.

But what makes me remember Junior forever is this: he brought me a gift when he returned. It was a filthy, single nylon leg cut off from a pair of panty hose. He said it would help make a powerful tea; herbs brewed inside this stocking would cure you of anything and give you perfect health. *Cures everything*, he promised.

We stood outside the house with its still unfinished work. I accepted the single magic stocking that unfurled and flapped in the slight breeze like a tiny shadow of a perfect leg, as he limped off on his missing one; and I did in fact remember him by it, remembered him limping and fretting about *them* and *the powers that be*, and wondered at the other, missing life—the potential, the phantom life, what was once supposed to be but had never existed.

The phantom limb that aches where the physical limb once was is "not a memory . . . of something now absent" but "quasi-present. It is the refusal of an experience to enter into the past" (Grosz 1994: 89). And there are plot fragments here that ache like phantom limbs, the resonating of something that lives on in the imagination, whether or not it once was really there.

## What Is "It?"

*It* is something real, though sometimes the only way to think about it is through its effects in story. The "it," the phantom object of the un-canny or fantastic story, never symbolizes a single "real" thing. Think-ing through the uncanny and the fantastic opens up the more general process of how narrative exceeds its literal, referential function to tell a "something more" (Stewart 1996: 5–6). The uncanny still demands to be read as true to some ambiguous but felt and embodied experience. It is presented and experienced as an actual memory. While the uncanny dismantles narrative conventions of realism and replaces them with uncertainty, its emotional force demands the listener attend to the teller with the same openness demanded by the genres of any personal narrative.

## Repetition and Resonance

Freud's (1963 [1919]) famous essay on the uncanny is best known for his insight that what seems strange is really the repressed familiar re-turning in a distorted form. It is the return of what we cannot bear to know.[2] But here, I want to focus on what Freud notices about its form. Freud says that the uncanny disrupts the ordinary flow of time when an otherwise unremarkable event inexplicably recurs, seemingly point-ing to an invisible agency or design through what he calls "involuntary repetition" (1963 [1919]: 390):

> We of course attach no importance to the event when we give up a
> coat and get a cloakroom ticket with the number, say, 62; or when we

find that our cabin on board ship is numbered 62. But the impression is altered if two such events . . . happen close together, if we come across the number 62 several times in a single day. . . . We do feel this to be uncanny and unless a man is utterly hardened and proof against the lure of superstition he will be tempted to ascribe a secret meaning to this obstinate recurrence of a number. (390–91)

In this passage, you see how the feeling of the uncanny begins to match up with a feeling about form. The events or images themselves are meaningless. It is when they are suddenly revealed as connected to each other in a single structure that their connection grows charged with the intimation of hidden significance, a "secret meaning," Freud says, or an intuition of relations that seem to be—somehow— purposefully constructed.

Freud's "secret meaning" invoked by repetition brings to mind Roman Jakobson's idea that the poetic function of language invokes our unconscious sense of grammar. Jakobson wrote that the poetic function of language foregrounds the "palpability" of signs with attention oriented to the message itself. It "deepens the fundamental dichotomy of signs and objects" (1960: 358), turning the major emphasis of the signifier from reference to poesis. Through "the reiterative figure of sound" (359) the flow of speech is "experienced as it is with musical time" (358; see Feld 1994: 190). The poetic function of language hooks reference into form, drawing on the unconscious patterns of language, and making use of them for a kind of meaning beyond reference. Jakobson's insight was that these effects occur through the poetic use of repetition with variation. Repetition with variation "projects the principle of equivalence from the axis of selection into the axis of combination. . . . Equivalence, normally the device of selection, is promoted to the constitutive device of sequence" (1960: 358). This is virtually a cubist insight; it's like the ineffable sensation of seeing your own bones in an X-ray. One of its effects in poetry is a feeling of heightened significance that transcends the referential sense of words themselves. In the uncanny, what might be thought of as "rhyme" or even "groove" (Feld 1994) occurs through repetition with variation with other stories and images. And in the uncanny, a similar experience of just-glimpsed parallels and heightened significance moves urgently toward its "something more," toward a just-glimpsed "secret meaning."

There is a *feeling* of a hidden "deep structure" that if seen in its entirety would finally make sense of the open-ended fantastic. The feeling of deep structure resonates in figures of an omniscient colluding government, or omniscient aliens, or a sense that an inexplicable synchronicity underlies seemingly random coincidences.

Anything strangely connected, any co-incidence, any pattern of events or images with an inexplicable meaning might have *something to do with UFOs*. If a member of the Hillview UFO Experiencers group where I did fieldwork got Freud's cloakroom ticket with number 62, it might have to do with UFOs. The UFO becomes a sign expressing that simultaneous sense of contingency and design, an inkling of some complete "grammar" of meaningfulness, intimated but finally ungraspable, felt lurking just beneath, or beyond, the glimpses offered by any single utterance. The parts resonate.

Metaphorically, one could think of narrative resonance as an intertextual half-rhyme, which in poetry produces a more ambiguous sense of structure than does full rhyme. UFO discourse shows how new forms emerge through the hybridization of elements from genres that, although discrete, also share some trope or theme, and some implicit, felt resonance. Resonance produces aesthetic intensity and the poetic pleasure of repetition with variation not only in consciously artful stories but also in the lived and embodied metaphors and the felt, discursive practices that compose phenomenological reality. Then resonance rushes into affect, "its impacts suffered or barely voiced" (Stewart 2007: 8). In ordinary life it's felt in moments, flashes. "The flashing up is real. It is delusional" (8).

*The flashing up . . .* I think of how, describing intertextuality, Richard Bauman quotes Bakhtin's image of the meeting point between texts as a "light flashing" (Bauman 2004: 4); it is an image that suggests the electric liveness of an utterance, dynamic at its point of coillumination. And in the stories here, the metaphorical flashing light between memories, utterances, or texts flashes with the beam of a UFO. The UFO is, in part, an expressive vehicle through which people poetically intensify and heighten the resonance between texts, and feel the flash of apophenia.

Talking about UFOs, people say: *Connect the dots!* They draw a structure that flows from the incidents; the structure is an effect of discourse about the "dots," but the dots never make a completely closed constellation. There is always another dot, another possible design.

## Connecting the Dots

One day Antony called with an urgent voice. (Again, this isn't his real name, and I have altered details of his story to protect his anonymity.) Antony was having intense memories of things he said he had edited out of his own mind because they didn't make sense. Now he had let them back in, with an uncanny sense of a sudden, returning image. And among other signs of the bizarre, he urgently wanted to tell me about his sudden memory of being a child and seeing a *dog's black eyes*. He said he was now *connecting* that image to pictures of aliens' black eyes. Not until he began seeing pictures of alien eyes did he begin to have an uncanny feeling of the dog from his childhood memory. Here the two sets of eyes, the ordinary and the strange, become parallel signs for him. They begin to form an irreducible montage in the image he produces; it's a picture in the dark, lit by resemblance. The iconic shape and color of the alien eyes intensifies—and disrupts—his older image of the dog.

In one sense, the dog comes chronologically first; Antony knows he saw the dog as a child, long before he ever saw any pictures of aliens. He says he saw the dog eyes before he ever saw alien eyes. Antony suddenly thought just now of the dog eyes *because* they looked like the alien eyes that he already remembered more recently, from years of noticing images of aliens in public culture. Now the remembered eyes of the dog suddenly are cast into the position of uncanny resemblance. They become the beginning or the end of a story (in inner speech, and then in a circulating story). Now it is hard to tell which comes first, the dog eyes or the alien eyes.

Now he wonders if it really *was* a dog he saw after all, back when he was a child. Maybe, he thinks, in both excitement and dread, maybe the dog was actually really an alien; and maybe the dog's eyes in his memory were really a screen memory for the black eyes of an abducting alien, the eyes he might have seen as the alien approached him. Maybe he was abducted as a child and blocked it out. In Antony's story, the resemblance between the dog eyes and the alien eyes is no longer sequential but instead enters into a relationship of combination. Their achronologic resemblance itself *makes* the ordinary image of "dog eyes" that popped into his mind suddenly uncanny.

In UFO discourse, people imagine a chain of semiotic association that is much like Freud's classic sense of repression as a chain of associations. First Antony thinks he forgot the real eyes of a dog. But maybe, Antony then starts to worry, maybe the dog eyes were the *false* referent; perhaps his own mind *invented* "dog eyes" to block out the alien, and then, since they were too similar, ejected them too. Now the dog eyes have come back, but what do they mean? Can you know for sure?

Antony worries over these looping chains of screen memory. But how could you not think, too, of what Antony does not say about eyes, given the phantom status of his own vision? He has been blind for years. He speaks of his old life with nostalgia and faint loss. Stories come out now and then. Once he was a father and saw his child born. He owned a beach house and got up at dawn to look at the ocean. He looked at his wife and saw his wife look back at him. Then he slowly lost his vision. He struggled with the eye disease. His wife *couldn't deal with it* and left him as he went blind, and his children were grown and scattered. But now he remembers from long ago something he'd shut out of his mind: seeing a UFO like a liquid light of every color, the size of a football field, over the creek bridge in Hillview. He was a boy, speeding along in the backseat of the car, gazing through the window up at the sky through the open hills. He *edited it out* before, he says, no one in the car with him talked about it. His father was in the military. *Notice, Susan, how often these things come around the military,* he adds, and in his family—well, it was a military family, and they didn't talk about the *weird things* they saw in the sky. But yeah, they all saw it.

Now decades later he remembers the black eyes of a dog, silent, looking at him. Why would he even *remember* that, he says again. Who would remember, all of a sudden after decades, something so banal and ordinary as the eyes of a dog? Why would it haunt him, why would it even have a place in memory, if it *wasn't* really *something else*? And come to think of it, where would that dog have even *come from*? A dog just appearing in memory, out of nowhere? What was the context? What was this dog, and why is the rest of the story gone? By the end of our conversation he says, it must have been a UFO.

His own eyes are blind and his vision is a missing thing. But, he says, if he hadn't gone blind he wouldn't have been open to seeing *this other stuff*. Other stories always get inside, opening the final grammar even wider.

In the Hillview UFO Experiencers group, people cultivate apophenia. Apophenia is the experience of seeing patterns or sequences in random data. But who says what is random? We open our hands and throw seeds of apophenia into the ground we've already prepared. Some of them take root, grow, become living things with repeating patterned branches. It is exciting to be making patterns we've privately known come forward in talk, to be making them the base of community. When it was my turn to speak at the UFO Experiencers group, I talked one day about my *weird experience* of having many co-incidences with the number 333. When I got a laundry ticket it was 333, when I opened a book at random it seemed always to be that page, and when they issued me a student ID as an undergrad, there was the number staring at me. In my teens, I told them, I used to wake up a lot at 3:33, and when I did, my heart would sink with the dread of the half-dream state, before I looked at the clock. *Please don't let it be . . .* I would think, but then, it was. As Susan Harding wrote, these are "apertures in the ordinary" that can be "constructed verbally" with stories (1987: 79). In the group, from my place in the circle where apertures in the ordinary are continuously constructed verbally, I remembered youthful moments of open strangeness, when the dark would press against the window like the body of a creature and inscrutable patterns could come to the surface of things.

Here in the group, it was possible to say things you would never tell others outside more familiar registers of intimacy. I recalled the middle of the night, with the branches of the mimosa tree tapping my bedroom window and the uneasy feeling of a silent suburban house in which you are a child. The UFO Experiencers group supported me with silent and murmured affirmations, urged me to continue my story. *Yes, this was something that fit here.* I could talk about those 333s at any meeting and it was sometimes disturbing or exhilarating to put it into story, to make it social, to see it come alive beyond my own head.

Once in a particularly strange encounter, I told the UFO group one day, when I was a teenager at a Talking Heads concert, a strange boy came up to me and told me out of the blue that *he* woke each night at 3:33. I could hardly believe it; I asked him why he was telling me this, and he said he did not know, that he had never mentioned it to anyone else. The group listened and took it in. Then other number pattern stories started to emerge from other people. One person woke up at 11:11, another at 12:12. They talked about what it was like to keep seeing these patterns. The woman who woke up at 11:11 also had strange things happen on November 11, 11/11, every year. Someone figured out the difference between all these times was yet another uncanny number in an old magic book. Lenny added some of the numbers up, and got the number of a local state highway; we realized that highway was a place where many UFOs had been seen.

The number story creates the poetic effect of a rhyme, a repetition with variation, a combination, a parallel. And so an underlying order, a "paradigm" or "grammar" of meaning is intimated. First there is my own, lurking in my own private stock of *weird things*; and then another pattern emerges, and accelerates my own memory into the shared, patterned, circulating field of the social. There was an immediate assumption in the group that our private numbers, added together, would get us closer to the larger pattern. For repetition with variation produces not just a sense of formal aesthetic pleasure, but even more seductively and urgently, the intense feeling of meaningfulness, the engine of uncanny discourse's social life.

But what did it all mean? I wondered, as I often did, as I drove Louise home from a meeting. She talked tonight about UFOs and the powers that be, she talked about the endlessly conspiring *them*, and the sky looked stranger than it had before the meeting when I was driving alone, the clouds hanging lower and wilder, with a presence that intimated some portent or significance. I wrote that night in my field notes, "All the way home she talked and talked about UFOs and finally she exhausted me; how can she keep thinking about this all the time, what keeps her so endlessly compelled? . . . No one in academia has this much intense intellectual energy as they do in the UFO group . . . but when she talks the sky looked stranger and stranger."

There were many other things that among these friends remained unspoken. Some of the most delicately unspoken was the stuff of personal lives you'd talk about at other kinds of support groups. But what could be counted on for story, here, was the urgent drive away from the arbitrary cul-de-sacs of the ordinary, always a drive toward a feeling of the *something more*.


## Repetition and Paralysis: The Poetics of "Something More"

A two-part trope appears in many stories here, mutating in a variety of incarnations. You can see it in stories of rootedness and transport, paralysis and flight, emplacement and wandering, and convention and disruption. All these are iterations of a structure of feeling I want to explore here, a recurring motif that keeps trying to tell us something.

This tension in this trope suggests something of the dynamic tension between Bakhtin's centripetal and centrifugal forces, opposing energies that occupy utterances simultaneously: "Alongside verbal-ideological centralization and unification, the uninterrupted processes of decentralization and unification go forward" (Bakhtin 1981: 272). The trope I'm talking about incorporates what was, centuries ago, narrated in American colonial encounters with alien others as "captivity and restoration." It's what contemporary American conspiracy theorists call on the one hand *independence* and on the other, sometimes, *being caught* and sometimes, with a lump in the throat, nothing at all.

You can be caught, captured, paralyzed, immobilized, stuck. You can be released, restored, redeemed, mobile, free. The tension between those oppositions produces a shifting image that always contains both of its own ends. Captivity narratives in general spin upon it. And the two antithetical poles—captivity and release—construct a third term, which is born in the meta-awareness of the relatedness between them. This metacultural glossing becomes a discourse; it circulates and lives (Urban 2001; 1996).

In this light, captivity—whether in stories of alien abduction, or women's Indian captivity narratives, or the nagging, embodied feelings of being trapped in myriad unspoken, class-inflected ways—is a countertheme. It is both opposed to and contained within dominant discourses of American freedom.


## Stuck

I met Stephanie in a different UFO community from Antony's. Stephanie shrugged her shoulders on the question of UFOs. She said, *If you think about it, I'm an alien, you're an alien, a Mexican or a French person is an alien, and that lizard over there is an alien*—and she laughed. Still, she had a way of narrating the events of her world into mysterious agencies and uncanny synchronicities.

Stephanie was in her twenties when her husband died, and the way she told of his death created a web of meaning. (Again, this is not her real name, and while I retain the meaning of her story about uncanny coincidence, I have changed some of the details in the interest of her privacy.) She gathered up the signs, and there was the pattern. Each sign was a little story, and each story layered up with the others into apophenia and resemblance. Stephanie said that right before her husband died, another relative died, all of a sudden, too. That made two untimely deaths, each layering into the other, forward and backward. It charged each of the deaths with meaning. It was the doubling that made the fact of each death not just a random event anymore, but *weird.*

She says: *They came in and there he was, just lifeless.* I ask about his death but she ignores me to continue with the real story, the story of co-incidences.)

At the relative's funeral, they had dream catchers for him and the goat skin on the dream catcher turned bright yellow and that was *kind of weird.* Someone said dream catchers catch your soul. And when they released the balloons into the air, the balloons made a heart shape in the sky; and then all of a sudden a white dove flew right through them. And the dead man's little daughter said: There goes my daddy, flying through the heart.

Well, said Stephanie, that was *kind of weird.*

Then after that, Stephanie's nephew died. Another strange death adding to it all.

She went to his casket and *said her good-byes* and she felt like *that was that.* It was time to start a *new chapter in the book of my life,* she said, and *this chapter was here* in this new town.

Then one day, here in this town, Luke, a young man Stephanie and I both knew, died in a freak car accident. The night it happened, Stephanie was just sitting in a chair and for no reason at all, a picture of her dead husband practically flew off the wall. That was *kind of weird,* she said. The next morning we all got the phone call about Luke, and she understood: The falling picture was the sign of her dead husband, comforting her, caring for her and protecting her. Letting her know: *She'd been through enough.*

Stephanie hadn't lived here too long, a couple of months. She had come to stay with relatives, to get away from hard times back home. She thought often about leaving here, going back to her hometown. And suddenly, as she began to consider moving away again, a bunch of people who had also just moved here began having car trouble, all at the same time. The multiple cases of car trouble layered into the multiple deaths and resonated with them, and became part of the web of apophenia.

And Stephanie said:
OK, I haven't quite figured this out yet
but it's like there's something and it keeps me here.
That's why I can't get my car fixed.
My water pump went out when I went to go pick up Kelly in
    town.
My water pump decided to go out in my car.
OK, ever since then, we have been trying to get a water pump
    to fit that car.
And we can't find one to fit it . . .
But for some reason,
we have exchanged that water pump
now four times
and four times now
it will not work on my car.
So there is some unnatural force keeping me here.
It must be something good or it wouldn't keep me here.
I usually don't stay where there's nothing good.
So there is something keeping me here causing this *time warp*.
The car situation with everybody—I think that it's all *con-
    nected* in a way . . .
Because if you think about it, we've all become so close to
    each other . . .
So even though we all come from *the same thing*,
it's like we were brought together for a reason.
Susan: What do you mean by *the same thing*?

And Stephanie mentioned the problems and tragedies her friends
had recently experienced before moving here, the spirals of falling
through middle-class lives into hardships and crises. They discovered
they all used ways of earning a living on the edge that no one wanted
to return to.
    *We all have something in common.*
    *We all have something in common, in an unusual way.*
Stephanie and I were just chatting, sitting in the house doing not
much of anything, and this story wasn't told in a traumatized or
haunted register. It was on the level of uncanny small talk, a free-
floating bit of speculation on the ways of the interconnected world and
its unseen forces of agency. In the play of ordinary events, there were
some kinds of extraordinary forces that simultaneously produced

Stephanie's own immobilities and put her in the center of a story that was larger than what we could see from our places on the ground.

First there were the terrible events—the deaths of three people close to her, including her husband, all in a row. Their proximity in Stephanie's life made a pattern, a story with an open end. The fact of all the deaths was strange, but the strangeness was made significant by the signs that they left, the traces you could see in their passing. The dead lightly haunted, left tracks of their continued presence. Balloons, falling photos. The ghostly signs showed their mourners that the dead were present at the funeral.

She told those events without much feeling, because it wasn't that kind of conversation, and we did not have that kind of emotionally intense relationship. We were friends, and she often told me the most personal things I could imagine . . . but they were not really disclosures in the sense I was used to. They were perhaps signs of the fact that she had lived, in fact, through a lot of trauma, and she told things that sounded terrible in a way that was emotionally contained. She told them as if these were simply her stories—the things that had happened to her. And she could tell them without expressing vulnerability, without making them an automatic passage to an exposed interior self. Instead they always opened outward to other stories, into senses and intensifications that exist outside, inexplicable but meaningful, part of a pattern.

Here, after Stephanie tells me about the series of deaths, she tells about being caught in a new town, about a *weird force* that traps you. The water pump itself "decided" to go out. "Something" is keeping her here. In this tiny, informal fragment of story Stephanie performs it all with a lot of verbal repetition, as if to mimetically enact the structure of the uncanny message itself; if you try to hear her words out loud in your mind you can hear the repetitive thud of the cadence, how it emphasizes the built-up weirdness of normal things:

My **water pump** went **out**
when I went to go pick up Kelly in town.
My **water pump** decided
to go **out** in my **car.**

And: . . . to get a water pump
to **fit** that car.
And we can't find one to **fit it** . . .

And: we have exchanged
that water pump
**now four times**
and **four times now**
it will not work on my car.

In a sense, she verbally constructs a mimetic little "time warp" of
her own in this most ordinary of anecdotes. She is foregrounding combination over sequence in her narrative. Inside that little formal time
warp, I didn't really know whether she *wanted* to leave or not, nor
whether it was frustrating to be here. This is a way of talking that does
not try to explain the subjective emotional experience of immobility,
but instead draws on the force of the paradigmatic. It poetically emphasizes the redundant, and shows the story's own ability to circle back on
itself instead of moving on. It reiterates the structure of immobility in
its form.

And that bit of story leads her directly to the next *weird thing*: that
her new friends are trapped together here, unable to escape because
*something* is keeping their cars from moving as they should. They are
as close as siblings, as she told me, because of yet another uncanny
recurrence: the common, traumatic life narratives and abject ways of
getting by that they have found they shared. What they have in *common* are the parallels emerging between unique lives, in stories of
homelessness and addiction for some, and making a living in ambivalent sex work or other small-time marginal ways for all. There were
hard times before they came out here and shook it all off.

But they didn't shake it all off. They didn't move all the way on.
Through its co-incidence, the *common thing* is still trailing them—
like a phantom limb, or like a phrase, repeated in inner speech till it
becomes something else. It's still there, what she again repeats as "the
common thing, the common thing." Yes, she says, we all have it, the
common thing.

She says their *common thing* is "unusual." It is unusual enough
that its recurrence is meant to be uncanny. The common thing, the
way they lived on the edge before coming here.

And so perhaps that *thing* is not just a sad past, but the index to a
*something more* . . . something that is not just the life you did not
want, before you threw it off to try to start over in midlife. It is also the
fact that—and you just know it on a hunch—maybe the terrible things
that happened in life took place, in part, because of larger structures

and patterns. Maybe the wounds you suffer are caused by paradigmatic forces and powers beyond what you can see. There is a reason that in lives that know economic struggle without cushions of support, *things that happen* as a matter of course seem to repeat themselves in different families from different towns. Across different lives there are resonating backgrounds of addiction for some, sex work for some, and of loss for all. And all these things occur against and within the ubiquitous American master narrative of freedom, the prescriptive for personal independence that is supposed to be a staple and a birthright as well as an expectation to live up to. The captivities, the containments, and the immobilities in these stories form a continual counterpoint to that larger saturating story of freedom and endless personal choice.

In these stories of being banally, uncannily stuck, there is a hunch that maybe it's not all your own fault. There is a hint at what, in other discourses, might become a sense of political and economic structures that impact lives beyond sheer individual choice. There is a recognition here that you are indeed caught in a structural *something* that extends beyond your own choices; there are things in the world other than your own "personal responsibility," although that master narrative of personal growth and potential clashes always with the sense that you were somehow *caught.* Stuck.

So maybe there is a real reason she can't seem to move. Something *out there* is bringing these friends together here, and it's holding them in place. This place. It's not just your own agency that's gone bad, and it's not random luck that creates the spiraling plot of your story. But what that *something* is remains mysterious—wide open.


## And There's Nothing I Can Do

Again and again you hear it in UFO worlds: I was paralyzed, I was immobilized, I was shut off, I simply could not move.

So now I want to tell you a paralysis story about trauma with an open-ended referent that is never going to resolve. The ambiguity is *itself* the generator of meaning.

One day, some friends from the UFO support group and I were sitting around the table at Tom and Carl's South Hillview place: Tom, Carl, Tom's wife Sharlyn, and me. (I'm changing their names here, too.) We were passing a guitar across the table, drinking beer, joking and teasing, and as always we were telling stories. Carl got us all singing

Neil Young—*Well I dreamed I saw the silver spaceships flyin in the yellow haze of the sun* . . . My tape recorder was turned on, covered with cigarette ashes, the cats half-sitting on it, pretty much forgotten. And then, Tom sat up straighter and told this story:

Did I tell you about the time I woke up in the middle of the night and I was paralyzed. And there was two objects. I say **objects** because they were not human. One of them was at my head side, another was there by my midsection. . . . The one that was towards my head had a thing in his hand. Called a *wand*. It had a green light at the end of it. And I couldn't move, I couldn't do anything.

So I was watching him, he took this wand, put it by the top of my head like that and my head started tingling, [Tom makes high-pitched pulsing noise] just tingling from the top of my head and started moving it *real slow* down my head, and down my body. And as he moved it on down, the area at—between the wand . . . started to tingle.

And my brain going wn-wn-wn-wn-wn-wn-wn-wn—Have you ever heard a dynamo?

Susan: nnn-nnn [no].

Tom: It's loud. It's mighty loud—dynamo—it's a *power-*producing unit. It's round, it spins, it spins. Like a genera-tor. And it produces a lot of noise [louder] wnwn**wnwnwn** that's what—inside of my brain. It was going **wnhwng-wngngnggn**. Like a dynamo! But my body tingled—outside my body. And I couldn't move. And as he [the alien] went down, the point between *here* and where he started to tin-gle, the rest of it was, nothing happening, and as he went down, that area from here to there would tingle and vi-brate. And my mind would go **whangwhangwhangwhng-whngwhng.** Electronic dynamos in my brain.

Got about to my knees, they quit. They pulled it away and my whole body was just, *whng whng whng* from my toes to my head. Just sitting there vibrating, whng whng whng whng. Like a vibration in my system.

Sharlyn laughs (uses a suggestive voice): I wish I was around. (Laughing.) . . .

Tom (ignoring her) Now, they disappeared. *Pssshhht!* They were gone. I remember laying there, and the sun coming up, and I can see light starting to come through the windows, and there's about an hour, and I finally managed to get up and walk around. But just trembling, and the vibrations still on my skin and inside my body. It was about an hour to an hour and a half before I could finally settle down, really move around naturally. I couldn't before that.

Susan: You were a kid at the time, or an adult?

Tom: I don't know!

I just remembered it! It just came to me one day all of a sudden boom, memory just start popping into my head.

Susan: Wow, so you'd forgotten for a while, and then it just popped back into your head?

Tom: I remember the gas heater up against the wall, that produced a light that lit up the room because of the fire . . . a low light, I can see things there. . . . They're there. And they're doing things to me and there's *nothing I can do about it.*

What can we say about the place of *the real* in a memory like this? First, I notice the intensity in Tom's voice. It is painful to listen to this story on tape, even years later. The confusion of the real adds to the discomfort, for the experience itself is a real experience, a phenomenologically real, embodied, and felt something-that-happened, whatever its source might be (Hufford 1982). The experience here has returned, possessing Tom as he tells about it. His voice is creaky and low; it sounds injured. The immediacy of feeling in his voice suggest no buffering lapse of time between the event and its retelling here. If ordinary narrative constructs the past as stretching clearly behind the moment of storytelling, this uncanny time is different. Tom's urgent voice performs his feeling of some unmediated experience. It seems not that he wants to *represent* that experience in an ordinary sense, but to create an immediate *presence* (Armstrong 2008). The aliens are summoned to presence by the story, and they begin, through performative language, to occupy the room with us. There they are; in the present tense, he says, "They're there." In the present tense he says, "There's nothing I can do about it." And we feel it. Even with Sharlyn's attempt to defuse the discomfort with humor, we listeners are caught up in the troubled feeling Tom's story conjures into the room.

This telling seems to speak a kind of set-apart memory, outside of normal time. It performs the hypnotic power to collapse discrete borders between an original "event" and its recollection. It collapses the distinction between the form and the content of narrative. There are multiple collapses enacted here. At the height of the story Tom describes his body this way: "the area where he started to tingle . . ." Is this "he" the alien, who is actively "tingling" Tom's body—an unusual use of "tingling," like tickling—or is the "he" Tom himself, disassociated, seeing himself from the outside? This kind of pronominal ambiguity happens in times of disassociation, in trauma or trance (cf. Urban 1989). Sometimes in that altered state you see yourself from the outside.[3]

In the shifting terrain of the real, Tom's embodied feeling of powerlessness is the one bit of terra firma. The more Tom is objectified by the aliens, the greater looms his own embodied subjectivity in the narrative. His feelings and sensations swell up to fill the whole space of story. The entire scene is mapped onto the subjective points of his own body. The structure of the narrative follows the linear path of how the alien sensation itself travels along his body. In contrast, the "outside" circumstances—the "setting"—are ambiguous and liminal, set in the indeterminate space of bed during a late-night awakening. Are we to take it as "a dream" or as "real?" The irresolvable quality recalls Todorov's sense of the fantastic, whose reality is never resolved one way or the other. The fantastic "occupies the duration of this uncertainty" (Todorov 1977:25). In Tom's story, after the invasion is over, the room returns to focus—the heater, the light. Before that, everything had vanished but Tom's body and the alien wand. In the absence of any signposts to grab onto, is Tom supposed to understand "paralysis" as caused by alien technology, or by his half-dreaming body unable to move?

This in-between paralyzed state of uncanny or alien encounter has been described elsewhere (Hufford 1989; Adler 2010; Clancy 2005). But here I focus on how, as with any trauma anywhere, the feeling of dissociation still arises from the conflict between *"They're doing things to me"* and *"There's nothing I can do about it."* As with any trauma, we hear about the enforced passivity of violation, the rage that has nowhere to go. And that is a sensation that does come and go, in a myriad of unspoken fleeting moments that are immediately sensed in tiny ways, and then put back down.

And so perhaps even the most inexplicable, fantastic, uncanny traumas that seem to mediate between waking life and dream do articulate with unspoken injuries, the subtle ordinary traumas whose pervasive violations and sense of disempowerment sometimes start to seem like the air you breathe.

I am not saying that the uncanny simply "represents" or "symbolizes" those everyday times. Rather, we can see a domain of associations, resemblances, patterns. There are hints, in the stories we do see, at yet another structure. The forgotten attracts the forgotten.

But what can you make of all this? You could focus on the immediacy of technological imagery: the sound is not just (through simile) "like a dynamo," but it *is* "electronic dynamos in my brain." Tom performs the part of the dynamo, the loud, obnoxious noise he can't "explain" but can reproduce. *Ever hear a dynamo?* he asks, and then throughout his narrative he embodies that sound, he becomes it, and creates the presence of its invasion. Here you might think of the way technology appears in UFO discourse. Aliens have greater technology than humans; this is their power. Technology in UFO discourse is opposed to nature, to feeling, to the body. Sometimes the aliens are forces of technology run amuck. They can't feel anymore; they are like futuristic robots, drones using a terrifying technopower to subdue and claim what they've lost, the natural bodies of humans. And sometimes the aliens are here on earth precisely because of the dangers of our own technological excesses; we're going too fast, we're going to blow ourselves up, and the earth is a ruin beneath our dangerous high-tech things.

But though the dynamo is a bit of technology, it is neither a terrible nuclear bomb, an inscrutably knowledgeable computer, nor a mysterious DNA splicer. Rather it is an element in a field of familiar signs that point to working-class labor. It is one of the tools that are used by bodies in an ordinary realm, the realm of work. The dynamo is a "power-producing unit," in Tom's polysemous words. It produces power—human power, the power of wealth, and the ordinary but (now that you think of it) mysterious energy of electricity that runs invisibly through the natural world, waiting to be harnessed and concentrated through specific modes of production. What's uncanny, here, is how the homely tool reverses its ordinary function of "producing power" for unmarked human use in unmarked relations of power, and becomes, instead, the means of intensified human subjugation.

Csordas (1993) describes charismatic Catholics taken by the spirit whose supernatural sensations are physically much like Tom's but experienced in a much more positive way. Thinking about their intense encounters with spirit, Csordas points out that the body is the ground of both phenomenological experience and habitus. It is impossible to separate the feeling of the dynamo and the social meaning of the dynamo. And here the tool loses its place as an implement for use, and itself becomes a user of bodies: animated, enchanted, fetishized, magic.

And speaking of magic, you might notice the residual images of fairy tales here (cf. Bullard 1989 on the similarities between alien abduction and fairy kidnappings). Here, the alien strength occupies an indeterminate realm, transgressing the boundaries between genres of childhood fairy tales and modern industry. Tom says right away about the tool: "One . . . had a thing in his hand. *Called a wand.*" This last striking sentence implies that the "thing in [the alien's] hand" is *already* "called a wand" in some preestablished world of meaning, a narrative realm of fairy tales. An existing universe of objects is implied, in which things have names that evoke entire fields.

But this is not just a modern telling of a fairy tale. This story mimetically links worlds of "magic" and worlds of "technology." The "green light" at the tip of the wand carries the intensified power of dual association: it shines simultaneously with the archaic power of magic and the modern power of a generic technology, all shot through with the uneasy sense of the uncanny power residing in the laborer's tool.

None of these analyses is a final story. None of them "explains" the experience of the uncanny terror, although they do articulate with it. None of them is more real than the experience of abduction itself. It might be a dream, it might be a memory that just *pops up* with no single event ever established as a referent. But it is a real experience; the paralyzed moment between dream and waking is real; the floating memory is a real present thing, whatever it might point to. The signs of everyday life and sacred fading structures bleed inside the experience, altering the specific social shape it takes. What's real for sure is that it lets you feel the everyday as unnatural once again, with its dynamos, its power, its countless embodied moments of possession and immobility. But still, the sense of the uncanny will not be reduced to another narrative told in the conventions of realism.

For what you have to notice most of all is the emotion in Tom's voice—a voice so full of violation and terror that it almost overwhelms the listener. What remains constant—not reducible to any other sign but holding them all—is the terror of paralysis as a thing in itself, the being *held down*, the abduction of will in the overwhelming wish for motion, for flight.

The paralysis caused by trauma does not disappear with the end of the violent action. It remains a force of inertia, outlasting the original referent. It can dissipate into the ordinary, become a structure of feeling attaching to nothing in particular (Berlant 2011). And sometimes it resonates with other kinds of immobilizations, with both the static, helpless sensations that often go without saying in everyday life, and the immobilizations of uncanny abduction.

The classic modern scholars of trauma said the "greatest confrontation with reality may also occur as an absolute numbing to it" (Herman 1977). Trauma might often entail this frozen delay of one's reactions, and the repetition of the memory as it intrudes, full of belated affect, into everyday life. The sense of paralysis is repeated in the aftermath of the trauma, for instead of "owning" one's memory, the traumatized person is "in its possession" (Herman 1977: 5). The memory seizes you, descends on you; and the traumatized person herself becomes "the symptom of a history [she] can not entirely possess" (5).

Cathy Caruth (1995: 5) described the trauma's repetition as a terrible literality, a "nonsymbolic quality" that repeats the original violation; "this literality and insistent return which . . . constitutes trauma." Yet at the same time, the returning event, in all its literalness, is not integrated into ordinary experience; it is "marked off"; it "possesses the person" in an altered state; and therefore its truth, the reference of that literal memory, is an uncertain terrain, open to question both by the person possessed by memory and by those who try to offer therapeutic healing (Caruth 1995: 6).

But over the past few decades, Fassin and Rechtman (2009) notice, the idea of trauma itself became a discourse. The recognition of traumatic impact became a form of common sense. Legal and popular discourses moved from "a realm in which the symptoms of the wounded soldier or the injured worker were deemed of doubtful legitimacy to one in which their suffering, no longer contested, testified to an experience that excites sympathy and merits compensation" (5). Psychological insights made their way into public consciousness about trauma and victimhood; and people began to recognize the symptomatic connections between victims of a variety of traumas. And at the same time, as the idea of trauma emerges into commonsense spheres of everyday life, a sense of unspecified trauma is in the air. Sometimes, the referent remains unclear. There is the force of many injuries, none of which can be pointed out and fixed. And all of them deliver the same sense of paralysis and immobility, the feeling of being possessed by a force or a structure that mocks your own volition.

But that is also how Plato regarded the repetitions of poetry. Susan Stewart says an ancient condemnation of poetry was premised on the potential for "lyric possession," which threatened dangerous derailments from truth. For the ancients, the poet does not truly possess knowledge; rather it's the poet who's possessed, possessed by the muse. And the poet becomes a "ventriloquist" of sorts, throwing his voice into the listener and confusing boundaries between self and other. Susan Stewart writes: when "speakers speak from the position of listeners," they disrupt the unity of voice and self. The listener becomes infected by the voice of the speaker, and the speaker projects her voice into the body of the other." Uncanny talk also possesses its listeners, snakes into the blood.

## Resonant Conspiracies

Intricate hidden structures, traumatic abductions, and immobilizing powers are also the ground tropes for uncanny conspiracy theories. But what makes a conspiracy a "theory?"

When it comes to the powers that be, any conspiracy you find is always incomplete, always still a theory. Dean notes that the "conspiracy theory" is always "outsider-y," its connections discounted, infected (Dean 2009). Conspiracy theorists sometimes make new plots, which are then called "conspiracies." This is what happened in June 1996, for example, on Long Island, New York, when three men— "conspiracy theorists"—were arrested for plotting to murder several local Republican county officials by radioactive poisoning, then burn down and take over their headquarters. The conspirators were accused of stealing radium, storing it up in ordinary canisters, planning to sneak it into the local officials' homes. And the choice of poison, in this story, was another bit of poetic fallout radiating from the pervasive nuclear uncanny in Masco's (2006) sense.

The author of this plot was a former clerk with the county courts who had been retired at half pension for absenteeism. He had once run for a local committee office himself and didn't win. He was a middle-aged man who, like most antisocial plotters in this tale type, lived with his mother. She herself had died the year before of cancer, as news reports of this story were quick to point out. He was represented in the media with quick strokes as an iconic type, the "loner."

Local newspapers reported on the story frequently throughout that June, accumulating details of colorful American strangeness. You could read that he was the president of the local UFO association. That he had many illegal guns. He lived on the ur-loner street of small, tidy houses. He left the floodlights to his house on day and night. He believed the government was covering up evidence of alien spaceship crashes. He began to seem extreme to the local UFO network; they wanted little to do with him after he showed them a photograph he'd taken of a crashed UFO in flames, which they felt was a picture of burning aluminum foil.

But the woods were on fire. He saw a downed UFO in the blaze. Aliens had set the brushfires. Aliens would consume Long Island in fire. No one would listen. The government was trying to hide it, but he knew that they knew that he knew. And he knew they were going to kill him. So, it was charged, he was going to kill the government; he was going to eradicate the powers that be, in the available form they took—local suburban councilmen. Just as the aliens had set fire to his turf, he would burn the house of power with his own arson. Just as power had invisibly injured him, he would dose its local incarnations with the invisible power of radium.

He hired two friends from the UFO association: a convicted petty burglar, and an electrical inspector for the Defense Department. One of the men stole the radium, perhaps from his job at the military contractor Northrup Grumman. And the other tried to hire others to help in their task. The three became simultaneous heroes and writers of their own plot. It was another example in the growing genre of antigovernment intensity that was spreading in the United States.

This story is finalized by its depictions in the news with quick strokes, through signs that point to social class without having to name it. The quick strokes of this portrait evoke that familiar but unnamed class position whose liminal image presents neither the folk rootedness of traditional laboring bodies, nor the authority of privilege. Rather it suggests in an underhand way the vague unspoken shame of striving for cultural authority without born-to-privilege ease. Here are stereotyped figures, real but also storied, who break out into horrors of excess. This story evokes a double image: the villain is represented at once a purely individual deviant, and a typed figure of liminal class ressentiment. He is portrayed as both passé and futuristic-fascist. Here the Constitution is read as a fundamentalist text, and the rights of the citizen to pursue something called *happiness* are a raft in a dream of drowning.

The familiar social aspect in this story suggests always a split between the promise and the actual package, between the master narrative and the life you somehow got. It's a ghost story too, the story of lost potential that haunts the real, in the slippings and losses of a life. Here is a story of so-called eccentrics who are not, in fact, eccentric or decentered at all. The leader, for instance, strove and dreamed and tried to run for office before he sank back down, and his accomplice worked a low-level job for the Defense Department; but, from half-inside, their breakdowns, unfolding in the realm of uncanny loss and desire, mark points of implosion in the dominant order of things. And then, decades later, he becomes a hero of multiple organized UFO websites. (A grass-roots web movement emerged, protesting his treatment by power.)

As always in the uncanny, the foundation of the real is here a shifting ground. What's real in this story is the conspiracy theory's dense figuring toward meaningfulness among blanched-out histories. *Something is wrong*, but no one knows what. No one talks about power as class in these stories, nor as a national foundation of slavery and the genocide at the base of American colonization . . . but disturbing free-floating after-images of enslavement and colonization remain, gathering in distorted forms, in discourses from people with no direct birthright to those traumatic histories. These stories don't *explain* anything. They find cracks in the order of things, then wedge themselves into the cracks and shape them with the resonance of other stories.

On the sliding American uncanny landscape, the real is not what you can finally prove but what you *just know*—that aliens are burning the world in fire. Or that you are an alien yourself, or a hybrid. Or that you have a child out there somewhere who was tracked and ripped from your body. *They* are tracking you with an implant in your brain. *They* stole your eggs and sperm. *They* leave their signs in body scars that have no ordinary source. There are signs that won't close in on referents, in spreading terrors of invasion. One day you are pregnant, the next day that baby is just *gone.* They stole it. They take you out of bed while you're still sleeping. They put foreign things inside you— embryos and half-born thoughts—then rob them back. *We* can't see *them*, but do *they* see *us*; they know where *we* are at every minute of every day.

And I don't know *what's going on*, says Fern, but I know it is not right. *They* don't care about *human rights.*

These accounts of the body's inhuman invasion and the earth's unnatural violation open into more stories, conspiracy theories perhaps, which also unfold around omniscience and defilement. We are being colonized. And the government knows *what's going on. They* are covering it up. A few months before the group suicide of the religion known as Heaven's Gate in 1996, which took the Hale-Bopp comet as a sign of the impending end of the world, people across the country were calling late-night uncanny talk radio[4] to say: A comet is heading straight for us, and behind that comet is a terrible thing four times the size of our planet, a thing made of metal and mud and guided by intelligent eyes. It will swallow us up, and *they know; their scientists* have the data in secret logs. And *they* have underground bases filled with crashed ships. *They* make deals with the aliens. *They* offered us up as guinea pigs; *they* are watching and *they know*—until the alien *they* and the government *they* converge into an allegorically felt figure of unseen power and agency, an overwritten, unfinalized *they* who invade and track ordinary experience from oblique, omniscient heights.

The uncanny late-night radio show, hosted by Art Bell from his home in "the Nevada desert," flourished and became a hit then. Everyone knew his talk about the escalating signs of apocalypse, what he called "the quickening." When you turned on his show, *they* were outed in the voices of 4:00 a.m. insomniacs bursting with elaborate theories of the universe and signs of the world's destruction. They *know* the earth is whispering its last breath under radiation and piles of trash.

Look around. Listen to the news, the callers said, hearing their voice go out across a nation. You know we are in the midst of plagues. You know *they* are hoarding secret piles of bubonic plague to spread on the population. It's time to prepare. The frogs are deformed, born without legs, or with extra legs that are withered and useless. There are uncanny limbs that show what's going to vanish. They're crawling now from the cleanest headwaters. The pelicans are dying, because the fish they eat are poison. I heard the manatees are going, and the honeybees are dying out too, and soon the other insects will follow; and there will be no more food. The invasion is sneaking in the borders of the earth and penetrating the margins of the body with clinical ease. And *they* are building themselves mansions and resorts underground where they will be safe, and hiding the truth from us.

Fern was my friend in Hillview who got the feeling there was *more going on.* She started to *make connections.* She'd been getting restless and wary as more and more things she knew were becoming incorporated by *them.* She emails me:

"Dear Susan," she writes,

*there is so much going on that you have to be careful. Are you sure you want to find this out? They are devious and brilliant and work through lies and deceit. They were back in Biblical times, they caused the fall in the garden. Their greatest accomplishment is to convince people that they do not exist. I think they've taken over the world monetary and political system. These are the Rockefellers and Rothschilds and others so hidden we don't know their names. The thugs in this world who push us tax-slaves around and make laws that only apply to us—not to them. . . . They are using mind-control technology perfected through CIA programs . . . through TV, and movies—in Independence Day notice how everyone comes together and obeys the government. We are being set up for a fake extrater-restrial invasion. They will use the Blue Beam and other technolo-gies to scare people to death and make them accept world-wide so-cialism. World money will be issued and a global police force will enforce their orders. Yes, we really have been invaded, but since "they" are guiding the education system, the media and the field of psychiatry, they make the rules. Little people like me are discounted—I'm a crackpot. But this is what I think is really happening. Watch for a fake "invasion" . . . The ones who aren't fooled by it have places prepared for them in "collection centers" and new prisons all over. . . . This is scary stuff, are you sure you want to go any further?*

There are plot fragments here that left trails, the ghosts of peripher-ally glimpsed effects of power, desire, and fear. It was hard to know whether they illuminated dangers no one wanted to see, or whether, in all their intensified distortions, made those dangers easier to ignore.

## CHAPTER 3

# Dreaming the Colonized World

## *The Resonance of Captivity*

Once upon a time, a representative of the U.S. military went to battle against the charlatan power of alien magic. John G. Bourke, captain of the Third Cavalry of the U.S. Army, made an ethnological study of what he called "our savage tribes" over twenty-two years of his position in the territories of the Southwest. Only one thing was preventing the Native assimilation to white society: the medicine man's sleights of hand. In 1892 Bourke wrote, "Notwithstanding the acceptance by the native tribes of many of the improvements in living introduced by civilization, the savage has remained a savage and is still under the control of an influence antagonistic to the rapid absorption of new ideas and the adoption of new customs" ([1892] 2003: 1).

For Bourke, this antagonistic influence was the medicine man's ability to control the identity of Native people and keep them enslaved to the past. He concluded that taking savage children to live at the boarding schools at Carlisle and Hampton might eventually convince Indians to abandon the miraculous technologies of the medicine man and embrace the miraculous technologies of the modern age instead. Only modern "wonders" could compete with their resistant magic (with "these wonders" a category in which "ventriloquism" has the same weight as "electricity"):

It will only be after we have thoroughly routed the medicine-men from their entrenchments and made them an object of ridicule that we can hope to bend and train the mind of our Indian wards in the direction of civilization . . . teach the scholars at Carlisle and Hampton some of the wonders of electricity, magnetism, chemistry, the spectroscope, magic lantern, ventriloquism . . . then, when they return to their own people, each will despise the fraud of the medicine men and be a focus of growing antagonism to their pretensions. (Bourke 2003: 144–45)

In short, the savage youth would be kept at boarding school against his will because he was still ignorant of the good it would do him and his people; and in this captivity, he would be converted to the wonders of modernity. Then the native could return as a changed person to spread the good news. For he was already, though he did not recognize it, "our . . . ward": a captive who would not acknowledge captivity.

The narrative underlying the boarding school policy is a three-part story of removal, conversion, and return. It is, in essence, a policy informed by a naturalized instatement of a genre with deep American roots; it is a captivity narrative. It reminds us, first, that the captivity narrative often has a shadow story that accompanies it, the conversion narrative and second, that the American master narrative of containment and assimilation is itself an iteration of the captivity narrative genre.

An extensive body of scholarship has shown us that the captivity narrative expresses anxieties and desires about colonization, gender, and race. The genre has been compulsively productive from the beginnings of American colonization.[1] Often considered the first distinctly American literary genre (Derounian-Stodola 1999), it has for centuries organized a durable American mythos (Slotkin 1973). I use captivity narratives here, not primarily as a way to analyze a literary tradition, but rather as an entry into thinking ethnographically about connections that people make between less clearly marked experiences in America. Narratives of many kinds—in public media, and in throwaway moments of everyday life—elaborate the trope of captivity, worrying over the dialectic of freedom and containment, and revising how those terms relate to power.

This chapter, then, continues to describe and perform a vernacular poetics. I focus here not on the shape, history, or limits of the genre, but rather on the resonance that emerges as people create parallels between various stories and images, and as they use those parallels to theorize power. It emerges in moments of American metadiscourse about what people often call *the weird stuff* in the world: the inexplicable, the uncanny, the apophenias that point to a pattern and structure lying beneath the surface of things.

These narratives splinter into the two-pronged trope that is expressed sometimes as explicit captivity and its restoration, sometimes as a more amorphous containment and release. The trope poetically compresses a fluid structure of feeling as the seemingly oppositional poles of the dyad coinfuse and tear each other down. They show how *abduction* can be both a traumatic ordeal, and the seed of a larger flight.

The stories in this chapter themselves produce a layered effect that tells us something about the ambivalent, ongoing project of narrating American identity through conquest. To perform this effect myself, I tell captivity stories throughout this chapter and let them reverberate against each other. The sense of things here comes from iterations that build up, and the accumulation itself creates a larger story. The vernacular theory of power is performed in these resonating poetics.

Kathryn Zabelle Derounian-Stodola (1999) says captivity narratives dramatize a member of the political and social majority becoming vulnerable to a less powerful minority group. In part because of this implicit reversal, captivity narratives allow complicated power dynamics to surface along with the anxieties and fantasies that attend them. Most famously in America, the capturing "minority group" means Native Americans kidnapping white settlers—often white women. In their memories of encounters with alien and savage others, white captives, upon their return, justified Euro-American expansion. At the same time, from within their captivity, they sometimes achieved a kind of ambivalent liberation from the naturalized constraints of their own society's conventions (Castiglia 1996). Living as a minority among the captors, the captive could begin to imagine a *something else.*

When John Bourke wrote his ethnological expose of the medicine man, captivity narratives in which Indians captured whites had been flourishing in America for over two hundred years. When there was a scarcity of fact-based memoirs of whites in captivity, fictive versions rose up to fill the demand (Ebersole 1995), though both factual and fictive stories would bend to the genre's conventional sway. Even when understood to be authentic renditions of material events, the story of Indians capturing a white American was a clearly marked genre in popular culture—an explicitly entextualized narrative. From the beginning, though, as Pauline Turner Strong (1999) has described in depth, what was not so clearly texted was the counternarrative in which whites captured Indians. The events that never became a codified popular genre might have included, for instance, stories of early colonizers

abducting Indians and taking them aboard their ships. One of the catalysts to King Philips' War in 1765 (the context of Mary Rowlandson's
famous captivity) was the kidnapping by Massachusetts Bay colonists
of three Indian children.

John Bourke alludes to "recent deplorable incidents in the . . . Dakotas" ([1892] 2003: 451), which, despite "improvements" in moderniza-
tion, should remind whites that Indians are still savages. Thinking of
"incidents" in the Dakotas might lead us to recall Wovoka, the Paiute
from Nevada who as a youth had been adopted by whites. Wovoka's visions of Native revitalization were a catalyst for the Ghost Dance religion; that revitalization movement led to the massacre at Wounded
Knee. People were dancing the ghosts back into the world then; the
white settlers would vanish, the buffalo would fill the prairie again, the
ancestors would return, everything would all become whole again. That
is the famous dream of the Ghost Dance, later written into the dominant master narrative of progress and regrettable, but inevitable, loss.

Less famously, when Wovoka was four years old, a conflict erupted
between the Paiute and a militia of white miners at Pyramid Lake.
Hundreds of Paiutes were killed. It began when white traders captured
a couple of Paiute women. The experience of these female Paiute captives did not enter into the texted, genre'd world of Indian captivity
narratives. It was just another scuffle between savages and rough-edged
pioneering men. But the pervasive story of Indians kidnapping whites
became, as Strong puts it, a hegemonic tradition in Raymond Williams's sense, taking shape through a "radically selective" process of
making tradition (2000: 4). The recognizable generic form that we recognize as a captivity narrative emerged only as all other possible elements, experiences, and memories were excluded. And the exclusion—
the unspoken forgetting—itself made meaning as surely as did the
foregrounded story.

When the captor is the savage, the trauma of confinement is drama-
tized in the captive's experience. The captivity is a clearly marked ordeal, with discrete points that mark its narrative beginning and end.[2]
But when the captor is the state itself, then its acts of containment are
told through images of paternal or civic benevolence: health, sanitation,
progress, enlightenment. At the time Bourke's report appeared, the
Ghost Dance had already failed its desperate dancers; the massacre at
Wounded Knee had already taken place, the U.S. military had already
proven its physical power. Now, in keeping with plans to convince the
enemy of modernity's "wonders," Bourke was advocating no more

slaughter but a civilized containment of alien people: incorporation and conversion where possible and separation when it proved not to be.

Nor, of course, did a sense of genre accrue to the hegemonic form into which the white captivity narrative, and its accompanying conversion narrative, gently evolved: the state's self-proclaimed benevolence, its taking of wards. This was to be seen not as a story, but as a policy unfolding ineluctably in the realms of civilization and health, "wonder" technologies, the unfortunate but rational eradication of anachronistic savage ways via the containment of the reservation, and the boarding school. This kind of containment was not, of course, to be read as a constructed or entextualized narrative, shaped by selective omissions. It was increasingly just part of the progress of everyday life.


## Another Story

Once upon a time, aliens starting coming down from space to colonize the earth and abduct human beings.[3] They followed the bomb, and the bomb had changed what was possible to think (see Masco 2006). For some years before that, UFOs had been witnessed skipping in the sky, as the first news report put it, like saucers. When in 1947 one crashed in the New Mexico desert near Roswell, local people found the futuristic debris out in the desert: unknown metals that crumpled in a ball and then unfolded without a crease, and the men couldn't cut it with their knives or burn it with their lighters; they also found streamer-like parts covered by some kind of hieroglyphic code. Some say that right after the crash, the military came to people's houses in the night and warned them: you didn't see it, you weren't there, and keep your mouths shut. Then the official explanation was that what had been found was only a weather balloon. Later, people told of seeing alien bodies killed in that crash. The bodies were small as children, but strangely formed like terrifying radiation experiments with huge heads and weird hands.[4] (And later still, investigative journalist Annie Jacobsen (2011) believed that, in fact, these "alien" bodies were the result of Soviet human experimentation, performed in the wake of Nazi medical experiments, and made to look like existing American movie images of aliens.)

At the time Roswell was the only military base with an atomic bomber unit. By 1947 everyone knew the gruesome deformities caused by nuclear exposure. The bombs had been dropped in Japan, and the fallout of nightmarish signs had drifted across the ocean. But these weren't people found and covered up in the desert. They were aliens.

Some say the government shipped those crashed aliens out of there, first to Ohio and then to a secret place called Area 51 on the edge of the Nevada test site. *The powers that be* hushed it all up about the UFO.[5] Then *they* started working with the aliens. The aliens possessed technology so advanced it seemed to be magic. They were invading the natural borders of our bodies and our land. But human powers also wanted the wonders of alien technology to use in our wars.

The aliens began to abduct people, it was said, to harvest our reproductive material, to make hybrids between aliens and humans. And the powers that be gave the aliens a green light, but made sure that abductees would forget it all when they returned from their weird captivity. *They* let aliens do this, some people said, in exchange for the high-tech alien information we used during the Cold War. Abductees would miss what was taken from them (sperm, eggs, time, replaced by the vague feeling of invasion), but they would never know exactly what had been lost. *Let us think it was only a dream.* That was the story of Roswell; that was how uncanny captivity narratives planted their seeds, in a resonant collusion of invaders and the government, colonization and war, experiments on the body and unspeakable apocalyptic fallout, abduction and power, all taking root in the American southwest.

In Roswell, an industry grew around the secret of the crashed UFO like a pearl around a grain of sand. Movies, books, a huge internationally visited UFO museum, a few smaller UFO museums, a yearly summer festival that stuffs the town so full of travelers they spill into the desert, all centered over the decades on Roswell. A congressman from New Mexico named Steven Schiff appealed on behalf of his constituency for federal secrets of official UFO-related policy to be released through the Freedom of Information Act. My UFO group friends in Texas said: *He got the pages, all redacted, blacked-out passages everywhere so you can't read it anyway.*

Of course *they* don't admit it, my friends said. *They* were behind it all along.

One day at the Roswell International UFO Museum I asked a young woman selling souvenirs what the people here thought of the UFO obsession surrounding her town. She said thoughtfully, "Well, it's been good, since the bus factory started laying people off." The bus factory in Roswell closed in 2002. The military base at Roswell has also been closed, since the late 1960s. But Roswell is a big town with an air of cheerful industriousness in the middle of the rural desert land.

After the UFO museum, my companion and I strolled Roswell's main street, stopping in here and there to chat with clerks in shops, which, though selling ordinary household goods, also displayed little aliens in their windows. Some of the clerks had grown up around here. Others had headed to the desert from back east to be near the UFO action, or to meet like-minded people who were into things like channeling, Native American spirit quests, and healing rituals.

Who lived here, before the pioneers came? Who knew this land long before the Roswell military base opened and closed, taking jobs with it, before the UFO museum brought more jobs back again? Were they Apache, Navajo, Zuni? None of our UFO tourist brochures told us that. On the road out of there, as we drove north through the changing landscapes, we saw people selling trinkets from roadside carts. They sold things that together created an indexical field of the "American West": Indian arrowheads supposedly found in these parts, UFO guidebooks, alien dolls, pioneer old-timey tools, and papoose dolls of no specific tribe wrapped in cellophane, the faces pressed up against the plastic like stillborns. One cart had a hand-lettered sign: Friendly Indians.

At one point we drove out to the desert to find the famous Roswell UFO crash site. Walking off the dirt road into the hills, we were high-spirited until for some reason the air seemed to shift. The atmosphere became uneasy. Things seemed suddenly weighted with a kind of half-meaning. I felt the sense of an evaporated history, the disturbing absence created by one world conquering another.

## Captivities

The fallout of the still-open wound of Native American colonization and genocide drifts into space alien stories. Guilt and confusion and injury sometimes survive the fading of their overt material referents, become uncanny emotional tropes, float into varied patterns of discourse and experience, and give impact and weight to other stories about inscrutable power, and loss.

It would be a mistake to say that the UFO abduction story is symbolically "about" that single history of American conquest. Instead, I'm trying to show how the captivity narrative points to multiple other social memories; how bits of those other stories accrue inside its form, and create new stories with social and poetic effects. One way to think about this process is by considering narrative and poetic memory as a complex, shifting, and expressive social form. Marita Sturken (1997) says that memory dwells "outside a definition of truth, evidence and representations of the real . . . [memory is an] inventive social practice" (259). She wants to "rethink culture's valorization of memory as the equivalent of experience;" instead, she considers it "a social and individual practice that integrates elements of remembrance, fantasy, and invention . . . [memory] can shift from the problematic role of standing for the truth to a new role as an active, engaging practice of creating meaning" (ibid).

What might it mean that memory is not the "equivalent of experience?" On a simple level memory is, of course, imperfect, mutable; it cannot transparently represent objective events. But "experience" itself includes fantasy and imagination, even in the most materially grounded, well-documented event, and therefore Sturken's idea can go further. Memory "exceeds experience" also because it can transcend the individual "owner" of the actual experience. Once even a private memory circulates—as utterance, narrative, discourse—it becomes social (Bakhtin 1984; Urban 1996). It escapes ownership and becomes a living, growing, changing thing. Then even those who didn't "have" the original experience can still take in and "have" the memory, absorb it as a kind of inner speech—and can alter it, transform it, let it express new, latent meanings that outrun and distort the transparent sense of the original experience.

Take, for example, memory in the women's Indian captivity narrative. Written, first-person memoirs of white women's captivity by Indians were from the beginning channeled through and framed by commentaries of pastors and husbands, often absorbing their editorial voices and influences in ways the reader can't determine. Fictional captivity narratives are not always clearly distinguishable from "factional" memoirs (Derounian-Stodola 1999); and furthermore, even the most genuine memories may come to resemble their fictional forms. But there is more to think about: what if the haunting imaginaries of American colonization, its fears and justifications, its guilt and ambivalence, is a social and cultural memory that outlives the individual settlers who were captured by Indians? Then in new guises the narrative itself can remember (Stewart 1996) themes that echo and multiply inside it. The memory becomes explicitly social as it twists into uncanny forms, as its "authenticity is derived not from its revelation of any original experience but from its role in providing continuity" (Sturken 1997: 259). Then the continuous, overlapping elements resonate back and forth in time, with meanings that still can't rest. "Continuity" creates parallelisms that in themselves gain meaning at the level of metaculture (Urban 2001). At the dense point where the various stories overlap you can see *a real* that is more complete, more true to phenomenological experience, when it is piled up in a heap of other stories than when it sits on its own. The accumulation itself is part of the larger story. And that common element of truth is, in part, the endless struggle over power that keeps repeating itself in countless social dynamics over time, sometimes foregrounding gender, sometimes race, sometimes class. Sometimes the phenomenology of power can only be told in how its effects reverberate between many different social categories, many different individual memories, and between many different, deepening layers of historical time.

Thousands of women's Indian captivity narratives were published before 1880. But why would the social need for these stories remain now, long after the establishment of Native American colonization in America? In what sense is colonialism's hegemonic project still incomplete? How does it overlap with uncanny forms of captivity like UFO abduction stories? How can we see the ways in which they coalesce into experience that resonates in both fantasy and material life?

But perhaps that line between fantasy and materiality is too pat. The women's Indian captivity narrative was always caught up in fantasy and expressively displaced female fears of an "oppressive" dark wilderness to which wives were often reluctant pioneers (Kolodny 1984). At the same time, it expressed the tensions and inconsistencies within the master narrative of colonizing Indian land (see also Strong 1999, Ebersole 1995, Castiglia 1996, Slotkin 1973, Faludi 2007). Woman's Indian captivity narratives always allowed the American colonizing project to underscore other unmarked power relations, especially gendered ones, within white society itself. You could say that now, the Indian captivity narrative "occupies" UFO abduction narratives with all its ambivalent expressions about power. And I want to look at how other stories chime in with them, too.

Michael Sturma (2002) has methodically compared parallels between Indian captivity narratives and alien abduction stories. He describes, for example, each genre's theme of paralysis, noticing that the captivity or abduction entails being helpless, immobilized, stuck. Sturma quotes *Communion* (106), where Whitley Strieber, in a memory of his own alien abduction, describes himself as helpless and immobilized as an infant. Sturma notices that Euro-Americans captured by Native Americans use strikingly similar motifs and images, speaking of paralysis, helplessness, and a frozen ability to speak.

And although Sturma does not as explicitly recognize the pole of liberation that opposes this paralysis, he does recognize many points that you could think of—and that many abductees think of—as escaping containments of many kinds. He sees, for instance, that both historical "captives" and uncanny "abductees" begin to identify with the other side, sometimes to feel a liberation in the crossing over.

One thing is clear: the European domination of Native American land is an uneasy, still-unresolved, foundational master narrative. It's a legacy filled with competing ideologies, both guilt and glamour. It ambivalently ricochets from images of pastoral settlement (the perfect containment) to genocide (the keenest social entropy). The loose ends of that ambivalent dyad are still being woven into compulsive narrative meaning. When the image of *abduction* just seems to resonate inside fields of imagination and experience, then, I suggest, inchoate stories about some kinds of immobility are gathering momentum, even in their still-inarticulate forms. Mostly I think about the unspoken stories of class and its damages, both in the enormous, work-related damages to the body, and in the little everyday injuries that gather up in their own unsayable patterns. Together they shape a felt sense of the real. I want to suggest how tropes from "factual" captivity narratives collude with fantasy and personal experience. They generate uncanny, class-inflected understandings about being trapped, about escaping, and always about what some call the powers that be.

## Each Will Despise the Fraud of the Medicine Men

Being abducted by aliens can be so traumatic that one man has devised an invention to thwart it. Aliens use mind control and communicate through telepathy, and they have unimaginable technologies that leap through quantum logics of time and space, but at everyday physical commonsense tasks they are completely inept. A man named Michael Menkin (2003) created a thought helmet to physically block aliens from reading our minds. His extensive website takes you through a detailed set of instructions, over several web pages, from step A through step J. Here is the instruction from step A:

1. Hold the hat open and push the paper into the hat. Push the paper against the inside and top of the hat. A newspaper will do.
2. Take the hat with the paper in it and put it over your head. The paper should be just above your ears and flush with the front and the back of the helmet. Pull the hat and the paper down over your head. Make sure the paper and the hat are secure against your head.
3. Remove the hat and the paper, taking care to keep the paper with the hat.
4. Use a marking pen or grease pencil and draw a line on the paper where it meets the hat.
5. Remove the paper from the hat and cut along the line you just made.

> The paper shape is the pattern from which you will cut the 8 pieces of Velostat. (12 pieces if you use 4 mils thick Velostat.) NOTE: Minimum shielding is 8 sheets of Velostat 6 mils thick or 12 sheets of Velostat 4 mils thick. Some abductees report success with helmets using only 5 sheets of Velostat but 8 sheets are recommended as the aliens transmit a tremendous amount of energy. Use more sheets if you can get them in the hat. (Menkin 2003)

The instructions continue over the seven separate web pages of alphabetized steps, taking you through the proper cutting to the final application of tape (horizontal) and reminding you, at the end, to apply "tape to any areas that need reinforcement. Remember, you will sleep with the hat on" (Menkin 2003). On other areas of the website, there are photographs of the helmet's creator and other satisfied users, testimonials about how effective it is, and admonitions to wear it as much as possible—even "24/7"—since aliens have been known to take hats from closets (as happened "in Kentucky") and to interfere telepathically by making you put the hat away when you were about to place it on your head. The best defense is "to wear the helmet as much as possible" (Menkin 2003).

The helmet is a simple mechanical gadget, but aliens have spindly, flaccid fingers and a weak understanding of normal material properties. As long as you use plenty of sticky tape, aliens can't get it off your head. (Once my friend and I were driving in the desert and we saw a family standing helplessly by an overheated car. My friend went over and showed them where in the engine to pour water. What would have become of them, out there in the sun? My friend returned to our car and told me in an amused voice that the stranded father was a physicist at the university, but didn't know how to put water in his engine. In a way, the aliens' helplessness with the tinfoil thought control helmet is that kind of story). Menkin would know where to pour the water.

Made from ordinary things, constructed easily enough by following the step-by-step process outlined in detail by the inventor, the helmet represents the modest, practical resistance of the human as a skilled craftsman, an ordinary working maker, protesting the invasion of an alien mode. This alien mode includes a focus on technological connections rather than goods, high-level and high-speed transmissions, and the unbearable power of its thinglessness. Here alien power is thwarted by the fantastic banality that the humbly constructed thing does, in fact, retain.

What I'm getting at here is the metaphoric poignancy in this helmet's bit of concrete magic. It signifies a protest, however fragile or marginal it might appear, voiced by the residual age of making a clearly usable thing. As with Tom's dynamo in chapter 1, here the invisible, untraceable encounter with the alien points to the charged mechanical objects; these are crafts and tools that flag a vanishing age of visible production. The helmet's power to block the alien depends on the value the workingman places on his craft (for Mr. Menkin insists he's not out for profits; he is not a capitalist, not an entrepreneur but rather a maker, sharing his bricolage for free with other like-minded abduction-resisters, his neighbors on earth).

In one sense, aliens conjure an image of postmodern power that seems to move in transmissions free of material constraints. It's a mode of power made manifest in connections and networks rather than in clear material production, a power that we are told endlessly accrues in "flows" instead of "goods" in the neoliberal age. And yet the helmet insists, with its precarious victory, the alien mode is still itself hostage to the vanishing power of the ordinary material thing.

Aliens have come here to earth, some say, to examine the concrete workings of our bodies. They take our literal sperm and eggs, the stuff of our innate power *to make*, to materially reproduce. And despite their ability to jump through time like quantum tricksters, *they still need that actual stuff*. For whatever their inscrutable alien ends may be, they *need* the fallible human body, much as any blindingly complex corporate system of information and power still needs, and takes what it needs, from labor. Someone, somewhere in the world, is in a factory making the microchips that *they* use to track us, as aliens track us. And aliens need sperm, eggs, bodies.

Here then is one captivity. The vanishing and the residual—the working but vulnerable body—is caught by the shock of the alien new and the seemingly immaterial base of its occult power (Comaroff and Comaroff 2000). Here on Menkin's website is a thing, a piece of handy making—a helmet—that seems to hold that alien power off with its own materiality, just maybe a bit. Its humble bricolage summons a structure of feeling that is still game but increasingly trapped. It summons something real that fights becoming a ghost.


## Ghosts

Once upon a time, I am watching a video on YouTube. It is 2008. The video is called "Indian Aliens" and its context is as opaque as anything else on YouTube.[6] You see only the face of an unidentified teenage girl who seems to be Native American. Her presence as a performer is strong: a half-submerged smile, hinting at without quite breaking into irony. The background paneling and couch suggests a modest home. She seems to be reading her lines from another computer off-screen.

The video begins with a tinkling sound, evoking "spaceships." Then the girl begins to perform with a spoken introduction:

> Do you think there are aliens waaaa-aaay out there in space?
> I don't know, buddy. All I know is, I'm not scared.
> Because I went to boarding school!

Soon, up comes a synthesized drumming. She nods along and begins to rap. She raps the desire to fly off with the aliens into space, leaving behind the "dusty res," the "tribal politics," and "the BIA [Bureau of Indian Affairs]." She will transcend comic annoyances on the reservation, such as a "crazy" local character. She dreams that the spaceship will fly her to a place beyond all this, a place where you don't hear about "soldiers killed today" on the news. She raps that even "Grandma" is planning to go; this Grandma character says that everyone in Washington "is drunk with power today." The girl raps that "grandma's put her spacesuit on," a spacesuit that was "banned by the BIA."

This spaceship is not the sinister vehicle of a clinical alien plotting to steal reproductive material with high-tech magic. Rather it is the vehicle of fantastic and transcendent rescue, taking Native people away from the captivities of ordinary existence and flying off to the "rings of Saturn with ease." Soon the performer modulates from the rap into a Hollywood-style iconic "Indian" minor key beat, humorously inviting all Native friends to "pack up your fry bread, and a brick of commodity cheese"—and to escape from earth *with* the aliens. These aliens are not conquerors, but rather a means to overcome the already-conquered world and its troubles. She emphasizes: "Boarding school survivors, you're welcome on this flight."

Next she shifts to a nostalgic recuperation of a past. The song now dreams a time before the "dusty res," before the BIA, and before the Indian boarding school, but nonetheless a past that takes place in the imaginary of outer space. The song dreams a time and place where all Natives might be united in "cosmic powwows, way out there in space." The image summons a comic, YouTube-era echo of the Ghost Dance. Maybe, the song muses, aliens in their futuristic spaceships will take us backward, back to a time before the plunge of things down to the way they are now. In this abduction there will be "no soldiers killed today," that is, no Indian kids signing up for a stint in the ordinary U.S. military; instead we will meet unconquered Indian warriors from yesterday, recuperating and revising the one war that really mattered. The song, then, comically dreams a time-space that revitalizes the future and redeems the past:

> And if we should go back in time
> I wanna see Custer there.
> Running' from the Indians
> Trying to keep his yellow hair.
> [Minor key Indian beat]
> Hey—ya! Hey—ya!
> [Spoken]:
> . . . No way, John Wayne.
> I'm not scared.

John Wayne and Custer appear together in this revised imaginary landscape. The cowboy actor who generated "fictional" characters and the "factual" cavalry commander of the Indian Wars are collapsed into the song's recognition of one, inescapable story. Abduction here is a narrative implicitly understood to be co-produced by both fictional representations and historical events. Inside the framework of alien abduction, the historical captivities of the American past become redeemed.

I wonder if she's written the song herself, or if it has circulated on Native networks on the Internet; maybe it's been passed from hand to hand. Some Googling lets me know that the performer is Inupiat, and goes to high school in Kaktovik, Alaska. But Kaktovik is not the "dusty res" that this song both embraces as a rooted place and wants to transcend. Nor is Kaktovik a place, apparently, where "fry bread" would typically be eaten (Fox, personal correspondence). But something comes together with these images: in a narrativized sense of historical Native experience, politicized and poeticized in its memory of Custer; in "dust" and "fry bread" as recognizable, representative icons of modern indigenous American life; and in the shared imaginary of a comic/cosmic revitalization. The white fear of alien abduction is nothing compared to the abductions of history. And so dread is replaced here by both desire and deadpan humor: "I'm not scared [of alien abduction], I went to boarding school."

Here, then, the real abduction narrative is the boarding school story, and the true captivity is on earth—not as a necessary spiritual condition, not as an irrevocable plot by supernatural aliens, but as a wrong turn in the contingency of the historical and the political. It's clear here that boarding school is an abduction too.[7] But the boarding school trauma inoculates its captives against the contemporary terror of alien abduction. In a small, jokey YouTube video, myths intersect and make a new story. The UFO—the ultimate sign of the other—here reverses and redeems the Indian captivity narrative, taking the earthly other into a chronotope of revision, revitalization, and redemption on YouTube.

YouTube viewers, unsurprisingly, leave their comments, some of which are meant to shock and sully in the commonplace way that anonymous, online misogynistic, racist, and blanketly insulting comments do. My heart sinks; I hope the girl does not read them. And after a while, the YouTube video is simply gone too. Did she take it down because of the comments? There is no way to know the story of its circulation or disappearance. It is another ephemeral object in the technologies of this world. I am glad I saw it, that I transcribed the song while the video was still posted; I am glad the lyrics are, for me, still *a thing*. The performance is, perhaps, now fittingly thought of as another ghost, resonating still with those who saw it after its vanishing.

## A Vanishing

Once upon a time, on November 5, 1975, in Arizona's Apache-Sitgreaves National Forest, seven men returning through the woods from a logging job saw a UFO descend from the sky and hover above the trees. One of the men, Travis Walton, got out of the truck to get a better look. And there in the Apache-Sitgreaves National Forest, Travis Walton, like generations of other whites in Indian forest stories, became, as his website puts it, "an unwilling captive of an alien race" (http://www.travis-walton.com/witness.html). He went missing for five days. Then he mysteriously reappeared, dumped back on a nearby rural road.

The story has been told and retold for three decades. This was the first abduction story told to me at the first major UFO convention I attended, in the early 1990s.[8] A UFO believer approached me and without introduction asked: *Do you know the Travis Walton case?* The question was phatic, a marker of community.

In this abduction case, Walton is zapped unconscious by the beam of light and wakens in the UFO. He thinks, at first, he is in a hospital: "There was nothing I recognized, but some of the chrome-like objects reminded me of those in a laboratory or doctor's office." That is what the UFO most looks like, a hospital or a lab, with rows of things that Walton calls simply "instruments," indexing a scene of "science." He sees the aliens approach. They are silent. They are hairless; next to them his own hair is a sign of naturalness, unruly excess. They have no fingernails either; the hands that clinically reach for him are pure white, with no seams or knuckles, as if their very hands have become surgical gloves, and it is as if their faces, which reveal only the eyes, have become surgical masks. But this is no hospital; this is a nightmare negative image of a hospital. Or, you might say, it is another example of how the uncanny partly reveals the hidden, terrifying aspect of knowledge and power in a nightmare of medicalized domination.

This hyperclinical nightmare articulates the implicit terrors of everyday life and its unspoken structures (see Brown 2007 for a thorough and insightful elaboration of medicalized imagery and the body in alien abduction narratives). The clean well-lighted space, the ordinary venue for containing trauma, becomes the generator of trauma. Travis Walton tries to smash up the instruments, he says, like an animal that has gotten loose in a lab. But, fantastically, or through the "wonders" of some new technology, nothing breaks. Here you might inevitably think of a

Foucauldian sense of medicalization. But here Foucault has fallen down a rabbit hole.

There is so much here, drifting from piles of memory and history, and settling into a story that tells an unfinished feeling about power and containment. There is the Nazi-influenced imagery—the nightmare of the medical experiment that drifts into UFO abductions from the very beginning, and then overlaps with images of atomic experiments on human and animal bodies; there is the oddly resonant idea of what Walton calls his own "superhuman strength of a trapped animal"—that is, the animal nature of the human compared with an alien. And so the "superhuman" element of the self here is not the brain but the body, which struggles and fights its captivity.[9]

Here is where the rabbit hole twists into a Möbius strip. It is not hard to hear the Indian captivity narrative layered inside this uncanny, unfinalized UFO abduction story like sediment. In the older story it is the Indian who is the savage, the devil, the wild animal, the natural man, the strong-bodied but, ultimately, technology-weak other. It is also the Indian who is the abductor. It is Indians who should appear in the forest and make you what Walton calls "an unwilling captive of an alien race." But here the Indian forest becomes the Apache-Sitgreaves National Forest (Barbeito 2005; Lepselter 2005); it belongs now to the nation. There is a knowledge trying to surface here, as always, that territory once belonging to Native people becomes entextualized within a Euro-American Indian place-name, an ordinary, unmarked sign of conquest. And in this contained forest, and inside the UFO, the abducting "alien race" is an intensified image of the white man: now this pale, high-tech, clinical alien race is descending upon what has become Walton's land, conquering what is in this narrative his native place, his earth. In terms of narrative identification, the abductee has traded places: once the captor was less technological, more "natural." But it is now the captive who claims "native" rights to the place being invaded—the earth.

## The Resonance of the Clinical

Once upon a time, Saddam Hussein was rooted out of his lair and abducted by the forces of the U.S. military. After so much pursuit and evasion he was at last a captive. A photo appeared in many newspapers and websites. The image went viral as it epitomized the

American triumph. It is still surfacing in individual images across the Internet.

In the 2003 photograph, Saddam Hussein is not being tortured or killed. When the journalist Daniel Pearl was abducted by radical Pakistani liberation group in 2002, the photograph that was circulated in the media showed him in chains with a gun to his head. It was an image full of pain and the knowledge of imminent death. His torture was obvious. A propaganda video released by the group was circulated on the Internet as well, showing Pearl being harshly interrogated, and then the terrible beheading.

In direct opposition, Saddam Hussein's photograph in American captivity shows a different kind of spectacle: the clinical display of the superpower. The compelling image shows Saddam Hussein being examined by a doctor. It was understood that the physical brutality in the Pearl image shows the captors' ability to kill. The display of the American force shows the superpower's ability to capture the subject at a deeper level. What is not necessary, of course, is a display of physical force, since Iraq had already, at the time of this photo, been thoroughly and visibly bombed.

But in the photo, Saddam Hussein's head is tipped back, and his mouth is open to a glowing wand, the light of medical inspection. The beam of light illuminates the inner tissue of Saddam's mouth, showing us the red, intimate vulnerability of the fallen dictator's soft palate. We look, with the point of view of the observer, into Saddam's face, and see not an equal or greater opponent; we see not an agent, but a patient. The doctor, in this photo, is the one with agency; he looks at his patient, but Saddam Hussein's eyes look off to the side, to some spot on the ceiling. Saddam Hussein has unruly hair and a beard. The doctor has a smooth, hairless head, smooth gloves, and a barely discernable face whose only distinguishable feature seems to be eyeglasses. In fact, this military doctor looks a lot like one of Travis Walton's aliens: bald, with any nails or knuckles invisible in surgically gloved fingers. He has amplified eyes, and a smooth garment without seams. He is examining the unwilling captive.

How might this image from a military invasion relate to so many previous scores of alien abduction images? We can't say here, of course, that anything was directly "copied" from anything else. These images pile up from such disparate domains. One image comes from a vernacular realm outside the unanimously agreed-upon real, while the other is from a realm of clear historical and political impact. But they arise nonetheless in a shared field of both latent and explicit signs. Despite the marginal cultural capital of Travis Walton's story, it is still part of the field in which our social world takes root and circulates, makes dreams and fantasies, becomes myth, and happens in real material life.

Everyone knows that modern aliens are clinical abductors. But one day, when I am doing research with a group of UFO experiencers, there is tiny moment of narrative negotiation. A woman tells about her alien memory. She summons the dreamlike image and presents it to the room, the thing she has felt slipping for decades between the ordinary memories of her life. She tells us this was not a dream, but neither does she insist it has some objective reality outside her own experience; instead, she carefully clarifies: *I'm saying I'm aware that this happened to me.* And she tells us she was aware that "beings," as she calls them, were doing something to her body. Another member of the group begins to put her story into its generic place from the standard accounts of alien abduction: he tells her the aliens were performing medical procedures upon her to advance their genetic mission. *No,* she says, *they were not. That's not what they were doing.* Yes, he assures her. They each take hold of one end of her story and pull for a few minutes while the others in the group watch. He tugs toward finalizing her tale into the well-known track of medicalized alien abduction; she pulls it back toward an idiosyncratic and open memory, a centrifugal story that resonates with too many details to pin down (Bakhtin 1981). Everyone listens; soon the moment between them passes. But this little negotiation over the memory's definition becomes part of the larger story.

## Another Story

The "first modern abduction," as people call it, occurred in 1961 with Betty and Barney Hill, an interracial married couple: "Most everyone knows the story of how Betty and Barney saw a UFO while driving through the White Mountains of New Hampshire late on the night of September 19, 1961 and were taken aboard it and given medical examinations by aliens" (Lawhon 2000). Like women's Indian captivity narratives, UFO abductions began in the East and then migrated west across the country. Now "most everyone knows the story."

The Hills' is the story whose narrative elements became the foundation on which subsequent abduction accounts could be judged by a growing body of investigators who wanted to align themselves with mainstream science and psychology. It was the origin story of the genre (Dean 1998). Serious abduction researchers, as they often designated themselves, began trying to distinguish what they considered to be real abductions, where narratively atypical abduction testimonials, especially those remembered without the benefit of hypnosis, were dismissed as "confabulation" (Jacobs 1992). It was sometimes said that the pure "wheat" had to contain clinical procedures on the body; other, seemingly wilder or less classifiable stories could be safely put aside as the "chaff" (Jacobs 1992).

As in the Hills' case, many stories that began to comprise the genre were forgotten and recovered to memory later. In these stories, memory itself became the subject of a secondary captivity story: memory was stolen away, converted in captivity with false images or "screen memories," then through the help of professionals, released. But even while memory was held in captivity, strange fears and feelings remained behind as traces. Detached from their own referents but pointing toward them though a dense field of semiotic distractions, mysterious signs of the trauma mimic the cultural process of uncanny memory itself. You could redeem the abducted memory-of-abduction by patching together the eerie hints and traces. Then, through hypnosis, the recovered trauma was funneled into a single narrative from the amorphous flow of impressionistic feeling. Through hypnosis the therapist could go into the scene of the captivity, taking the abductee along on an inner journey to relive the experience. The story, this way, became a codified type, and the teller's original amnesia of that story was one of its key motifs. Here you can see that the UFO abduction story is itself a trace in the life of the social, an uneasy sign pointing to a half-forgotten disturbance beyond the individual's story. In social life as on the body of an abductee, "horror leaves its traces" in strange, eerie events (Comaroff and Comaroff 2000). But what is that "something," what is that original horror?

Betty was from an old Yankee family, and Barney was an African American postal employee. The fact of their mixed race (unusual in a married couple at the time) is always a noted point of the story. It's not a detail crucial to the UFO abduction itself, but it is a crucial mark of specificity, a particularizing fact. And more than that, it resonates implicitly with the themes of race and hybridity in captivity narratives of the past, and abduction stories to come. In Roth's (2005) cogent analysis, 1950 space "contactee" stories grew out of white supremacist theosophy; the Hills' 1960s story represents a move toward greater racial optimism. He incisively calls the Hills' abduction narrative "the suppressed trauma of a mixed-race couple during the civil rights era" (Roth 2005: 61). (For more discussion of race and hybridity in this and other UFO stories see Roth 2005; Brown 2007; Barbeito 2005.)

Driving their Chrysler on a lonely road, the Hills saw what seemed to be a star coming closer and closer until finally it was no star at all but a UFO, and Barney could see strange "living beings" gazing back through the windows of the spaceship. Barney yelled, "We're going to be captured!" like a pioneer in an old cowboy and Indian movie. There was no way to escape: the aliens came closer and closer over the horizon, spread in a line across the road, and then they captured Betty and Barney near Indian Hill.

It's like a dream, with these signs poking up as iconic landmarks to remind you of a nagging *other thing* just offstage. (But what is that other thing?) It doesn't make much sense on its own, this trail of signs, each sign like a single ember that must have floated in from a bonfire burning beyond the frame. Each ember is a clue to the bigger fire that both launched and connects them. Take the story's place-names. Look at it like a conspiracy theorist would, stringing the embers together so your necklace glows in triumph. There are the White Mountains, there is Indian Hill, and the last name of the couple is also Hill, and the double occurrence of "hill" seems to factor each hill out and leave you with the resonance of the words "Indian" and "White" (Barbeito 2005 also notices the symbolic place-names in this narrative).

Yes, these are real names and real places. And yet thrust into the charged and fantastic narrative, with its constant begging for the reading of clues, the names become signs that underscore the theme of a troubled unspoken history. The words "White" and "Indian" might remind you implicitly of other, historically earthly, material abduction stories that are nested inside this strange one. As in Travis Walton's story, these place-names tell us, of course, not that these narratives are somehow texted by an invisible author making symbolic choices, but rather how ordinary, and yet how troubled, are the legacies of theft and desire in the ubiquitous, unmarked use by whites of Native American place-names in everyday life (see Samuels 2001). The abduction story partially marks these names again as explicit indices to a story of invasion. The abduction story lets both the historical and the fantastic story resonate together as a feeling.

Susan Clancy (2005) calls the Hills an ordinary couple and implies that they represent the typical couple next door, strangely ignoring the narrative disruption of an interracial marriage in 1961. The couple's mixed race status is, here and elsewhere, a detail that seems to get in the way. It might give an extra jolt of disturbance; it carries an implicit sense that race is part of a larger structure of things whose workings aren't always visible at the surface (Roth 2005 elaborates on this theme). And then, when you think of race, the missing time also half-evokes a kind of "middle passage" in a spaceship. Its bewildered passengers are immobilized with invisible, uncanny chains; they remind us of other terrors, as they dread leaving their own world and becoming the possessions of these technologically dominating others. Different troubled American histories layer up inside the uncanny iterations, the implicit feelings of their parallelism between other histories of violation, transport, domination, colonization. They are unresolved injuries spewing back in a layered poetics, revealing the connections and parallels between many different histories of power and domination.

As signs, the place-names point to *a something*; and on one level at least that something is the apophenia in accumulated stories of invasion. In the dreamlike story of alien captivity, the polysemous quality of signs begins to pulse with the uncanny light of meaningful fluke. The details seem to refer to something urgent but obscure. Weird, isn't it, a white guy at a UFO group might say—because in many social worlds where people think together about UFOs, the work is piecing together the apophenia in things, the coinciding motifs in everyone's memories, dreams, books, road signs, numbers, and seeing a pattern. Weird that the first abduction was at a place called Indian Hill. After everything we did to the Indians. "We were like aliens to *them*," I have often heard UFO experiencers say, speaking of colonizers coming to America. "We invaded their land." Or: "When the Spanish came to the New World, no one knew who they were either." Here, in this musing analysis, "we" are the Indians in a native land, and the familiar patriotic origin story of the discovery of the Americas has shifted.

Barney Hill died an untimely middle-aged death. He was haunted to destruction, said some of the people I knew, by his irresolvable trauma. But Betty lived into the 2000s, a salty New England lady who made appearances at UFO conferences and was periodically interviewed about her abduction. Shortly before her death, her local newspaper in New Hampshire interviewed her again. The reporter Dennis Robinson was clearly delighted by Betty's eccentricities. But what she said surprised him. His story recounts that Betty is growing tired of representing the mystery of UFOs. She tells him she does not want to be known as the abductee any more. She brings out her research. She is studying her own genealogy now instead of UFOs, and is completely immersed in an old family story: she wants the reporter to know that one of her Pilgrim ancestors was captured by Indians. This is what Betty Hill wants to be known for, instead of her alien abduction: the Indian captivity narrative lying dormant in her genealogy of abduction stories.

## More Stories

Mary Rowlandson's captivity narrative from 1682 is generally considered the "origin" of the American captivity genre. In the seventeenth-century Puritan captivity narrative, it isn't clear from the text itself that Indians are well on the way to becoming a defeated minority, or that the war that is the context for her abduction resulted from the flooding in and domination by the English in one generation. Castiglia (1996) says that as Rowlandson fears for her life in captivity among savage "hell-hounds," her symbolic position of power within an official agenda of racial and cultural genocide must be reconciled with her lower status, within her own society, as a woman. But these implicit ironies grow closer to the surface later on in the American colonizing project. By the nineteenth century, when centuries of genocide had already cleared the way for folklore and nostalgia, you can read a gap opening up between what is known and what has been more obviously obscured.

In the earliest captivity narratives, the moral structure of things is cleaner. Mary Rowlandson, abducted into unknown wilderness, begins to explore what becomes a spiritually unknown space, conquering the threat of despair and her own vulnerability through the various ordeals of her survival. Her sense of God's intervention at each juncture under-lines her position as a stranger in a strange land. She has entered an otherworldly journey; and the point of her own narrative is the journey of her soul, which has to emerge on the other side of an odyssey filled with demonic perils, tests, and moments of divine grace.

In a sense, even though she's surrounded by savages, she's alone with God and her own soul; and the Indians (rather than truly seeming to have their own autonomy) are like figures in a Dante-esque crossing through spiritual darkness. Their representation has been read as "de-monology" expressed in the "imagery and folklore" of captivity narratives, a set of motifs which "pre-dates the Puritans considerably" and continues beyond them in representations of alien others (Ramsey 1994).

The poetics of these stories is striking. She recounts her children being murdered in what, for the modern reader, is an irreducible voice, where sparely stated facts seem to carry compressed enormities of emotion. For a modern reader, this stalwart condensation often heightens the shock:

> Two of my younger Children, One Six, and the other Four Years old, came in Sight, and being under a great Surprize, cryed aloud . . . the Indians to ease themselves of the Noise [made by the younger child], and to prevent the Danger of a Discovery that might arise from it, immediately before my Face, knockt its Brains out. I bore this as well as I could, nor daring to appear disturb'd, or shew much Uneasiness, lest they should do the same to the other [child]; but should have been exceeding glad had they kept out of Sight till we had been gone from our House. Now Having kill'd two of my Children, they scalp'd 'em (a Practice common with these People, which is, when-ever they kill any English people, they cut the Skin off from the Crown of their Heads . . .) (Rowlandson 1999).

This voice, simultaneously electrified by horror and resigned to it, says in the deep fabric of its expression that the ordeal is part of a plan heading towards God's ultimate redemption. For the modern reader, it is an unknowable consciousness which, having watched her children's brains "knockt . . . out" and then "scalp'd," admits only to wishing that she "should have been exceeding glad" had those children kept out of sight until she, their mother, had been captured. You might say this voice compresses sentiment into its own distilled poetics of intensified containment. After two weeks of caring for a suffering child who was wounded in the raid, Rowlandson simply reports that one day: *It did cry for Water until it died.* The Puritan captive struggles to maintain a pious voice as she recounts her own physical suffering through cold and starvation while resisting terror, estrangement and abject loss by focusing on God and the commandment to avoid despair.

Everything here signifies a real beyond itself, for early colonial captivity narratives took seed and grew within a larger climate of seventeenth-century stories, testimonials that matter-of-factly incorporated accounts of the supernatural, and stories whose strange manifestations could easily be compatible with truth claims. "After all," wrote Richard Dorson of the narratives of this era, "America itself was hard to believe, and the borderline between strange fact and colored fiction could not be neatly staked" (1950: 5). Part of a deeper social and imaginative zone in which the strangeness of the expanding world was part of God's creation, "the whole tradition of the medieval bestiary with its fabulous zoology, and the natural history of the ancients strewn with the incredible, lay behind the descriptions of the early travelers" (Dorson 1950: 5).

And therefore it's worth noticing that in Dorson's comprehensive collection of early American writing, among the marvels of strange, New World beasts, and unbelievably survived "accidents" involving spikes to the head; among the terrible enchantments of savage magic, and the ongoing, palpable struggle for God and salvation from the devil's incarnation in Indian flesh—there comes also from Cotton Mather this story, understood generically in his own time as a "true tale."

Once upon a time, Cotton Mather (whose father, Increase Mather, wrote the introduction to Mary Rowlandson's narrative) told his flock about a sign in the sky of an unidentified flying object. He wrote that he had heard from the "pen of the reverend person who is now the Pastor of New Haven" (Mather quoted in Dorson 1950: 161) that a ship bound back to England had not returned the following spring. The New Haven pastor wrote to Mather about something strange: "REVEREND AND DEAR SIR [wrote the pastor]: In compliance with your desires, I now give you the relation of that APPARITION OF A SHIP IN THE AIR, which I have received from the most credible, judicious, and curious surviving observers of it" (161, emphasis in the original). "Reader," confesses Cotton Mather, "there being yet living so many credible gentlemen that were eyewitnesses of this wonderful thing, I venture to publish it for a thing as undoubted as tis wonderful" (161).

And so here is a seventeenth-century airship off the coast of New England. It is an object that begins its flight as "unidentified" but resolves into a clear picture of a ghost ship. It is carrying the souls of voyagers returning to the Old World from the New World. The colonists return to heaven in clouds of glory, in an echo of Revelation that seems to solidify the spiritual standing of the colonies so far from their English home. Here, already, is an American narrative in which an otherworldly flying craft haunts the ambiguous process of crossing worlds.

You could say that the voyage across the sea to the New World was already an image that shaped the imaginations of those who later headed into the West, into the new world of the territories. You might also say that the vast sea was something like the vastness of space, into which, a few centuries later, ventured astronauts. From that space came new incarnations of ghosts, alien creatures, and new stories of captivity. But while UFOs are always forever unidentified, the colonial flying object here is quickly identified. First of all, it is defined: it is an apparition. Second of all, it is a direct copy of the known ship. Unlike the modern UFO, which indexes the unfinalizable, this sign has a clear referent. And unlike ghosts that haunt profane realms, ghosts in a religious context often have a singular referent (Gordon 1997); the direct link between signifier and signified speaks of an orderly world. The airship is, without "hesitation" (Todorov 1975), incorporated into a tight fabric of conventional cosmological and semiotic meaning. This haunting, then, is not disturbing or disruptive. Rather it is a marvelously affirming sign of God; and thus Cotton Mather justifies "to publish it for a thing as undoubted as tis wonderful."

Nineteenth-century women's Indian captivity narratives can evoke a different world from Mather's and Rowlandson's. The language of the journey into savage territory becomes more lushly emotional, more oriented towards the ambiguous. A different aperture for the uncanny opens up. I certainly don't claim to explain centuries of changes in uncanny American sensibilities, but it is worth noticing a few differences that are most salient here. In the seventeenth century, Mary Rowlandson's narrative was a constant reminder of faith. Although nineteenth-century narratives also testify to Christian faith, they emerge in a different context. Rowlandson's narrative contrasts in interesting ways with, for example, the narrative of Fanny Kelly, who was abducted by the Sioux in the mid-nineteenth century. Fanny Kelly had been captured with her young daughter, and in the midst of the forced journey put her child down in the tall prairie grass, telling the little girl to hide until someone back to fetch her. But then:

> In the morning when permitted to rise, I learned that she had disappeared. A terrible sense of isolation closed around me. No one can realize the sensation without in some measure experiencing it. I was desolate before but now that I knew myself separated from my only white companion [her little girl], the feeling increased tenfold and weighed me down with its awful, gloomy horror (1990: 56–57).

The "awful, gloomy horror" gives everything a surreal tinge. The Puritan captivity narrative represents good and evil, and the natural and the supernatural, as forces that exist autonomous of the soul who encountered them. But in Kelly's nineteenth-century text, these forces bleed into an ambiguous, unknowable subjectivity. It is Kelly's painful memory itself—not a ghost that lives independent of her affect—that becomes an agent of haunting. Her perception is saturated by countless other gothic texts, whose projection into an uncanny meta-image is indistinguishable from her own imagination. Her intimate memories become uncanny at the moment of their loss. They are pictures and sounds seen in the moment of becoming externalized ghosts. They are powerful as images because they are, like many uncanny things, "condensed" (as she puts it). In a traumatic moment, she superimposes this "condensed" essence of the familiar upon another "picture" from her inner stock of images—this one not an intimate personal memory, but rather the recollection of what she calls "some weird picture" from the world of publicly available signs, which has shaped her only way of seeing the alien, and that floats up to entextualize the immediate scene before her:

> In an instant a lifetime of thought condensed itself into my mind. I
> could see my old home and hear my mother's voice . . . the hundreds
> of savage faces, gleaming with ferocity and excitement around me,
> seemed like the lights and shadows of some weird picture" (ibid.: 61).

When Fanny Kelly was abducted by Sioux (this was in 1864), she was, in general, treated well, and at one point was cared for as a guest in the house of Sitting Bull. But the experience was agonizing; her husband fled the raid, leaving her, and her young daughter, Mary, was indeed killed as Kelly feared. On an unremarkable day later during the captivity, riding on horseback along with the Sioux on what "seemed to me an endless journey," a Native man she did not recognize rode up beside her. She writes: "At his saddle hung a bright and well-known little shawl and onto the other side was suspended a child's scalp of long, fair hair" (Kelly 1990 [1871]:141). Although she had already known that her little girl Mary must be dead, now she saw the girl's scalp, the hair separated from the person, and the empty bit of clothing whose "well-known" familiarity fills its shape with uncanny horror. The detached length of hair dreadfully summons up the image of the whole child. The existence of the part intensifies the nonexistence of the whole. It creates an inner spectacle for Fanny, who fills in a vision, now, with how that detached hair came to be removed. The familiar shawl conjures her child's absent body, and makes that absence palpable as a ghost. These disembodied parts lend a sense of phantasm that perhaps even seeing a whole corpse could not do. "As my eyes rested on the frightful sight I trembled in my saddle and grasped the air for support. A blood-red cloud seemed to come between me and the outer world and I realized that innocent victim's dying agonies" (ibid.). Unable to endure "the torture" of seeing her child's scalp and shawl, Fanny faints, dropping "from the saddle as if dead," in a "merciful insensibility [that] interposed between me and madness" (ibid). When she regains consciousness, her captors, having guessed "the cause of my emotion," have removed the scalp and the shawl from her sight. While she is still ill with agony, they bring her some "ripe wild plums which were deliciously cooling to my fever-parched lips" (ibid.) But the traumatic sight of her daughter's scalp and shawl produces further ambiguous, uncanny effects. Soon she can't even let herself know whether the "frightful vision that had almost deprived me of my senses" was a true memory or not. "I began to waver in my knowledge of it, and half determined that it was a hideous phantom like many another that had tortured my lonely hours. I tried to dismiss the awful dream from remembrance . . ." (143).

When Rowlandson's children die, their mother describes being grief-stricken. Despite temporarily "converting" to "Indian" habits during the liminal phase of her captivity (such as relishing Native foods she would have disdained before experiencing the hunger of her journey) Rowlandson never narrates the kind of ontological vertigo that two centuries later, for Kelly, rips into the uncanny feeling of the haunted. Captivity results in transformation; part of the drama is whether the captive will emerge strengthened or irrevocably damaged. Rowlandson struggles with sinful despair. In Kelly's nineteenth-century narrative, it's no longer her soul, but her sanity, which is in peril. Did she really see that terrible thing, or was it a dream? She would take comfort believing that seeing the scalp was just an "awful dream," if only that didn't mean she was losing her faculties. If Rowlandson's soul was tempted by despair, Kelly's mind is tempted by a sinkhole of madness that overwhelms her sense of what is "real" with "wild belief":

> I seemed to hear the voices of my husband and child calling out to me. Then I would spring forward with the wild belief that it was real, but later would sink back again overwhelmed with fresh agony (ibid.:63).

Over time, American captivity narratives open up to this semiotically ambiguous orientation of the uncanny. The demons are no longer part of the Puritan world's determined supernatural elements. Here the uncanny emerges as a struggle between the rational and the haunted, between the clearly known and the unbelievable. And it is connected inevitably to an absence: to an inchoate sense of a larger story that is not being told but is leaking into the picture—to a "missing time" that becomes inner speech and inner spectacle. A very similar sense of ambiguity about the real is a major theme in space alien abduction narratives as well. Did the abduction happen within ordinary material reality, or was it part of a different, more numinous real?

The form taken by any uncanny narrative is part of its time and place, an element in a whole fabric of everyday chronotopes (Bakhtin 1981); and the specific tone that emerges is inseparable from other social and narrative influences. You could trace a multitude of historical threads that weave together and come out to the same haunted destination in the end. It's true that, as Dorson points out, religious practices changed, and with them vanished the unmarked acceptance of otherworldly forces. But it is also true that in the nineteenth century, white settlers, even at their most vulnerable, felt the overall balance of power between whites and Indians shifting, as colonization marched on, as the war against Indians increased, and as new fields of meaning arose in its wake.

An ambiguous nostalgia is already in place, and sets the stage for a sense of haunting that permeates the trauma in Kelly's narrative. In the intimation of vanishing, the imagined Indian became less a figure in a powerful Puritan demonology than a symbol of new ways to access spiritual worlds. Later, Native religion is popularly portrayed not only as an aspect of black magic or evil witchery, but more frequently as a positive spiritual alternative to be appropriated for white personal growth. At the same time that a rationalist discourse advocated eradicating Indian religion, for example, Shakers in the mid-nineteenth century invited hundreds of "unidentified spirit-Indians" and a thousand Chippewas to participate in their trances in upstate New York. The famous late nineteenth-century Boston spiritualist Lenora Piper summoned the spirit of an "Indian maiden with the unlikely name of Chlorine" to meet séance participants such as William James (Brown 1997: 162–63). To those "discourses of the vanishing" (Ivy 1995) that pricked the dominant imagination in the course of changing power relations between whites and Indians, you could add the nostalgic settlement of wild western land—land that becomes, of course, the fantastically texted landscape of both American colonization and uncanny UFO conspiracies, the "West."

## Sedimented Captivities

Once upon a time, in the early 2000s, a friend from the Hillview UFO Experiencers Group tells me about a show on the Science Fiction Channel. The TV station hired archaeologists to lead a group (mostly UFO researchers) on a search for buried scraps of the crashed UFO near Roswell. One of the amateur diggers was happy to see that the land here had not before been disturbed by humans; it was pure and pristine, so, he said, metal found here must be from the UFO. Then the digger noted that the team "bagged" some old Native American artifacts. Here was the narrative sediment of UFOs and Indians, layered, literally, in the Western soil.

> (There was a sense of presences, of life that had come and
> gone before all this. At once I felt the sense of an evapo-
> rated history, the disturbing absence created by one world
> conquering another . . .)

This is how uncanny conspiracy theory builds, sign by mimetic sign, until your sense of where you stand is multiple and simultaneous too—invader and invaded, captive and captor. It is true that much UFO talk cathects Native Americans, not as people with specific histories and politics, but as indices to a lost time when the earth was still unbroken, its relationship to humans untraumatized. One of my friends from the Hillview group moved to Arizona, in part, she said, to "be near Indians." I visited her there once and although she had not met any local Native American people, she had met other like-minded white people, a few who drew the aliens that came to them at night with strange faces like demons.

On one level UFO talk converges with other, New Age discourses that appropriate and attempt to commodify (though rarely with much financial success) some fabrication of the "Native American" as a pure, spiritual index to the sign of the earth itself, as opposed to the alien worlds of space. Both UFO believers and New Agers in general talk often about shamanism and the channeling of spirits from the uncorrupted past (M. Brown 1997). I was given a session in Hillview one afternoon by Mark, an alien contactee (as he called himself) who described chatting with Reptilian aliens in his living room. They come down through the ceiling that suddenly reveals it can open lid by lid like an eye, he says, and then, sometimes, the Reptilians play scrabble with him. *Scrabble?* I asked, dumbfounded. Well, yes, they like Scrabble, he said. It was a shock of the mundane into the unearthly, and yet Scrabble was, in a sense, a fitting emblem of uncanny poetics, each letter potentially doubling from one word to bleed into the next, building up in ways both arbitrary and designed. And it was these Reptilians who gave Mark the power to lead people on guided visualizations, to find their Native American "power animals." (When I closed my eyes as he instructed me to find a power animal, part of me would not cooperate and I could only see a chicken. Mark tried to help me find a better one like a wolf or dolphin by taking a purple, glowing electrified wand from a velvet case of instruments he said he'd gotten at a yard sale, and passing its slightly shocking, tingling tip somberly over the outlines of my head and body.) This healing was itself reminiscent of nineteenth-century spiritualist practices, and again, reminiscent of what Bourke called the wonders of electricity—and even of space alien magic itself, like Tom's paralyzing "wand."

Once upon a time, in Hillview in the 1990s, I sit with people who are deeply immersed in thinking about all kinds of uncanny experiences, and the talk drifts to speculate about possible Native ancestors. I am a graduate student doing fieldwork with UFO experiencers, most of whom are white. It is a time before antigovernment conspiracy theory has a mainstream political platform, before Fox News, the Tea Party, or the birthers. There is just an inchoate feeling of coming into greater focus, a sense that something isn't right. There is a feeling that something ineffable has been taken away. A few people say they feel they've got Indian blood, and of course many white Americans do have Indian ancestors they cannot name, untold stories of vanished but lingering white-Native interaction, thousands of specific episodes of violence, love and entanglement most white Americans cannot know in the erasures of colonization

That one day, in Carla's little living room, among the clinking ice in sweet tea, and the meanderings of the dog and the cat, and the hanging smells of cigarette smoke, our flow of casual talk about what we called *the weird stuff* again turned to Indians and signs of abduction. *I think I have some Cherokee in me*, said Nat. Brian spoke of indigenous South American people he's read about in a *Readers Digest* book, people from the Amazon who were warning us about the peril of the earth's destruction; *they* knew about the vulnerable and sacred earth, how we're destroying it. Brian says: *It sounds like UFO origins . . .* Then Carla told of the three well-thumbed paperback books she was reading simultaneously. She had learned from one of them that it was tribal people in Africa, the Dog Star People, who had discovered Pluto— not the European scientists who claimed to have found it all. Speaking of Pluto, Brian asked, have y'all noticed how bright Venus was in the sky right now? The meteorologist on TV said that was normal, but Brian wasn't sure . . . it could very well be a UFO.

One part of this talk occurs in the register of the autodidactical quest for truth, a register too easily dismissed by established intellectual arenas supported by cultural capital. From Carla's living room though, this talk is both the fabric of social feeling, the expression of intellectual hunger, and a way of saying that *somehow, something beyond what we can see has just gone wrong.*

Always in such seemingly free-floating, autodidactical, uncanny talk, there's a feeling of another kind of captivity afoot. It's felt in a kind of intensity that burns its way through that talk. Talking and talking, the words built structures and ladders, the way prayers themselves seem to make a presence in a little church. The words in Carla's living room and everywhere she dove into conversation tried to break out of some invisible, ineffable constraint. Therefore it is true that this sort of talk is never really *about* real Native people who struggle with racism or classicism or the fallouts genocide, nor with any of the other ordinary insults of life that you, too, know when you leave this set-apart world of uncanny talk. Instead it's about lost potential. It becomes part of a single field of disenfranchisement and cosmology, and it all gets wrapped up in talk of UFOs. Histories of colonization and the naturalized expectations of class come together then in a comprehensive structure of feeling and imagination, to combine in a unifying theory of power, of being trapped, and the potential for redemption.

Things are different now, people say; those long-ago aliens aren't necessarily the same little grays who take abductees now. Now, because of modernity and its violent thefts, those old, otherworldly secrets are mostly lost. In the twentieth century, the government conspired with these gray aliens so we could get their technology, some say. And so some people dream a connection with a world ripped out from beneath the feet of other people long ago. "We screwed the Indians out of their land and then we ruined nature," a woman in the group says. Now, people say, the clinical aliens are doing it to us.

People at UFO gatherings sometimes talk about how space aliens can be found in ancient Indian cave drawings, or how the Indians know the truth that goes beyond human experience. Someone hands me a flyer at a UFO meeting. *Do you have an interest in Native Americans, or maybe some Native American blood? It could be a sign that you've been abducted by aliens.* In UFO talk, as in New Age discourses, aboriginal peoples of the world can become a sign of potential recovery, of freedom from the captivities of modernity—pointing backward toward innocence and forward toward apocalypse or redemption. It is of course a vast trope of guilt and desire, emerging in various iterations from personal speculative chitchat to Hollywood movies like *Avatar.*

On one level this discourse is a familiar trope that romanticizes the other. It exoticizes and incorporates, and its drive to mimesis shuns politics and history (Taussig 1993). Sometimes this discourse conflates all "tribal" peoples into a spiritual synchrony. At the same time, the people speaking to each other here about the *weird stuff* in the world are not, themselves, the powers that be. They too are caught up, trying to trace invisible lines of power from some untraceable source. It is possible to critique the New Age discourse of appropriation, and at the same time, to think ethnographically about how the Hillview talk reveals a troubled American unconscious, an unstable desire born out of legacies of both colonization and class, trying, in the way it can, to construct and express a different point of identification—one that just doesn't feel at one with the material power of the world as it is. This imaginary wants to set up camp on the bank of the other side, wherever that might be, and hopes with real fervor there's some other kind of other source of power lurking there, some other authority and generator of knowledge, beyond the ache of the ordinary and beyond the powers that be.

The white UFO believers here would agree with the Native American "Grandma" character in the Inupiat girl's YouTube rap, the grandmother who sees "everyone in Washington is drunk with power today." But they wonder—who holds the strings?

My friend Randall in Nevada says it many times: *We are all enslaved. Don't think for a minute that we are not.* White men do not have a direct historical memory or line to the long continuities of American slavery. For Randall, the source of enslavement is too vast, too deep to point to as one single thing. He is compelled to try to understand *the powers* that he knows exist but that no one can ever really pin down. What he feels *has happened* cannot be solely linked, for him, to the legacy of American slavery that gives him his emotional metaphor, or just to colonization. It is not just the tropes of dreadful medicalization leaking in from images of Nazi doctors or pictures of animal experimentation, or mysterious animals cut in the desert like experiments, or the inchoate feelings of disempowerment in ordinary encounters with power when you don't have the cultural capital to feel at ease within them (see Lareau 2003). And it is not just his, or anyone's, youthful experience of the containments in hard times. He layers it up: the resonance that emanates from many half-remembered signs, letting him know that there is more to power than what meets the eye.

CHAPTER 4

# You Can't Repair History

*Desert Vanishings: Into the West*

Having followed our stories from the previous chapter into the American West, here we are, with its captivities and liberties, its settlements and expeditions, its ambivalent hybridites, and its ghosts. Here we are in this place that became "American" inside the grooves of dual master narratives. One tells of a federal government whose arms can stretch beyond civilization to gather up savages. The other tells of a land so far from the center that you can fall off the edge, without any civilization around to contain things.

Ordinary and uncanny discourses resonate with each other as people talk about power in a place that is already deeply entextualized as "The West." This chapter focuses on how ambivalent discourses of colonization, nature, and civilization shape both fantastic and everyday memories in a small desert town that marks the borders of government and military secrecy. In the stories here, history bumps up against inchoate experiences of the body and its encounters with inscrutable forces.

In this chapter I tell stories about life near Area 51, the geographic focus of uncanny American conspiracy theory. The high-technology military base, and its restricted airspace known as Dreamland, is part of the vast complex of the Nevada Test Site and Nellis Air Force Bombing and Gunnery Range. This is the where, many people say, *the powers that be* have for decades been hiding a UFO. This place is where military scientists used reverse engineering to deconstruct it, after it crashed in Roswell, New Mexico in 1947. Reverse engineering means the government scientists took the UFO apart and learned its secrets so we could use that alien technological magic in our own weapons.

But our own weapons often seem impossible too. Area 51 is also where the Pentagon developed unbelievable craft like the U-2 and the invisible stealth bomber, Cold War surveillance technologies and the Mach 3 spy plane. It's a place where sudden flights of warplanes glinting in formation against the bright blue sky steal the breath of "plane spotters," guys who move out here to climb the small hills and wait, patiently and quietly with binoculars, the way men elsewhere might wait with a fishing pole, to catch a glimpse of power.

It's the place where unregulated years of "dirty bomb" testing invisibly spread plutonium over nearly a thousand acres (Jacobsen 2011). For decades, the existence of this base was completely classified; now its secrecy wavers in the fading shadow of the Cold War. But still, Area 51 is a clandestine military and technology base, a loud secret that performs the uncanny spectacle of mysterious forces.

The *hidden UFO* sits in a multiply-texted terrain. It generates fabulous theories that resonate with more ordinary discourses of nostalgia and haunting in a troubled historical landscape. People shade their eyes and point in its general direction. *There is the UFO up there, it's hidden under layers of earth . . .* For hundreds of miles this base is surrounded by mostly federally owned ranchland, the half-buried scatter of rusted old mines, partly-intact stone walls marking off nothing anymore, and the bleached wooden skeletons of forgotten homesteads.

Rachel is the closest civilian settlement to Area 51. From Rachel, population about ninety, it's approximately 45 miles to the small, mostly Mormon town of Alamo in one direction, 110 miles to the military base town of Tonopah in the other. Through this spare, desert terrain a dense field of meanings emerges. The futuristic imaginings of UFO narratives blend here with both the open wounds of an imperial American history and with local values of everyday competence, community helpfulness, independence and skill.

As news of a secret military base and its rumored UFO began to circulate widely in the late 1980s, first in the news media and then on the Web, people began driving out from Vegas to have a look around. The town of Rachel was too small to show up on maps at first, but throughout the 1990s it became increasingly well known in popular culture anyway, both for its proximity to Area 51's forbidden power, and for the little mom-and-pop business that sprang up there in 1989: a UFO-themed café and bar called the Little A'Le'Inn.

In the late 1980s, Joe and Pat Travis were a local married couple who had bought what was then called the Rachel Bar and Grill. Over the years, passing between various owners, it had failed and been revived several times, riding the waves of a hardscrabble rural economy like any out-of-the-way little desert café. The Travises took note of UFO seekers coming through the area, and with sharp business instincts, they changed the name of bar to the Little A'Le'Inn. (They picked the clever name, Joe explained, because the café is *little*, and it serves *ale*. And, with the five trailers they put out back so UFO tourists can stay the night out here, it officially became an *inn*.) The Little A'Le'Inn quickly gained fame, both in the pages of niche paranormal magazines and in international travel media featuring quirky and quaint spots to visit on a side trip from Las Vegas.

North Las Vegas drops off into emptiness as you leave the city limits and drive north into the Great Basin, a deep-set, harshly beautiful terrain curtained on all sides by red-pleated mountains. Except for the town of Alamo, there's nothing much but scrubby desert for about two hours until you scale the heights of Coyote Summit. And then, coming down a curve, you can see Rachel: it's a scattered sun-glint of trailers along the left side of the road. People who live here describe the moment of descending Coyote Summit as a deep feeling of returning, a shared marker of home.

But a local sense of intimate emplacement grows entangled with other, inescapable inscriptions. While the federal government was trying to keep the public's eyes away from Area 51, the state of Nevada was stoking the commodifiable desire bred by high-tech military secrecy. In 1996, Nevada State Highway 375, the remote road running closest to Area 51, was named the "Extraterrestrial Highway" in time for Twentieth Century Fox's promotion of the film *Independence Day*, which featured Area 51 as part of the plot (Campbell 1996). At each end of the 150-mile stretch of desolate highway, the state erected standard green road signs embossed with white UFO icons and the words "Extraterrestrial Highway" in a font that looked vaguely 1980s "computer-modern." Tourists could find informational packets in manila envelopes stamped "The ET Experience," with maps of the area, information about rumored UFOs, and lists of all the local commerce you could patronize for hundreds of desert miles, from "Jo Ann's Country Cookin" to "Spaceship Full Auto Service."

The Little A'Le'Inn is a double trailer with an extension; Joe and Pat lived in the mobile home right next to the café. Outside, a sign hand-painted with an alien face is turned to the highway: *Earthlings Welcome*. Now the café brings UFO pilgrims and tourists from around the world into the remote Tempiute Valley. Across the road from the café you can see the remains of collapsed old mine structures, forms whose overdetermined outlines give shape to the amorphous desert expanse that quietly holds them.

In 1997, the year I met her, Pat Travis won an award from the state for bringing tourism into poor, rural Lincoln County, which previously had relied on small-scale promotion of old-timey outlaws, ghost towns, and the iconic pioneer past. Pat hung the plaque on the café wall, near a clock depicting Jesus with his hands outstretched, counting out minutes to the End of Time. And it often seemed out here that something *was* coming to an end. As the master narrative of the glorious pioneer past begins to fade on the allegorical landscape of the American West, the UFO story seems to rush in to take its place. It too soon becomes familiar, with its recycling tropes of conspiracy, the hugeness of power, and the rush of a future felt to be coming too fast.

Along with its glossy brochure on the ET Experience, the state's tourist packet contained a brochure about the Pioneer Experience, sepia-toned like an afterimage. These two pamphlets index overlapping metastories of Western colonization. The uncanny alien invasion resonates with the memory of historical colonization. But in the UFO framework, citizens of Earth were the natives now, conquered by high-tech alien pioneers from space. Or maybe they came from another dimension of time. In any case, now white abductees were colonized natives.

Some people say it's the alien colonizers who are now crafting secret treaties with the federal government, up there on the forbidden base. Others say the UFO *up there* is another spoil of war proving the power of an unknowable force: that *they* are the ones who captured the UFO, dissected the alien corpses for their own secret reasons. In all these stories, the desert here is filled with resonating, layered tropes in a colonized land. The Native people who had lived in this place were no longer visible in many of the small towns dotting ambiguous territories between ranchland and military bases of the West, but their traces were central to its identity. Individual Native Americans and families of various tribes lived as a minority in small white towns, connecting to local white families with various strands of marriage, kinship, or adoption. Paiute, Shoshone, Washoe live in tribal communities around the state. But here, the story of Euro-American colonization was becoming the story of space invasion. Here we see fallout from the unfinished accountability of historical human displacement, and ambivalent alignments with just what *the natural* might be, in the overwritten, lived-in, secretive, and militarized West.

At the Little A'Le'Inn, there is photographic evidence of UFOs on the walls. There are newsletters about conspiracy theory piled on counters and in magazine racks. There is a little gift shop area (shelves lining a corner of the café) filled with souvenirs: alien mugs, UFO statuettes, Area 51 T-shirts. Ronald and Eileen made most of these souvenirs out back behind the café; they had the tools they need on the converted bus where they lived and worked, often traveling with the seasons. A local artist painted areas of the bar with haunting alien faces and deeply colored UFOs; the look of his painting makes the place feel immediately original and expressive, foregrounding character. There is a much-used pool table, a couple of slot machines (this is Nevada; everywhere has slot machines). Out front, in the parking lot, you could almost miss a jokey yellow diamond-shaped sign with a black little alien silhouette: *Alien Crossing*.

This is a place where ordinary and the fantastic signs overlap. The uncanny conspiracy theory pamphlets piled on the shelves of the Little A'Le'Inn contain themes familiar to any rural libertarian with a long historical distrust of federal government. Conspiracy theory mingles here with the cadences familiar to any small-town talk. In a rural county, the Little A'Le'Inn functions more like a small-town diner or Dairy Queen than an internationally famous, UFO-culture landmark of Americana. It's a good place for neighbors who live long distances from each other to come and discuss county politics, to get an update on someone's health or animals or court case, to relax and crack a few understated jokes after a long day's work in the sun. Community meetings are sometimes held here in quiet hours. And you come to treat your family to lunch out after attending Baptist services at the little church here in town. Once a week there's a spaghetti supper just for locals; then you line up at the steam table and, over a casual, homey meal, talk with the neighbors you don't often enough get to see, when you live *out here*.

There are the long, quiet spells of any out-of-the-way café, the sounds of a few ice cubes in a glass, the click of a pool cue on a ball during a laconic game, or a couple of café workers wiping things down. Then into the quiet indoor space, from the glaring sun or solid darkness that lies behind its metal doors, come the tourists to look around, to buy a T-shirt and eat an Alien Burger, and sometimes to strike up a conversation with the locals. The atmosphere in the café can change as abruptly as the weather in the desert outside. On a lark or on a pilgrimage, travelers come here from all over the world. Their voices mingle with rural Nevada talk in a constant polyphony of discourses. Sitting at tables and at the bar, there's a shifting configuration of hired hands from the nearby farm; rancher husbands and wives; cowboys and down-and-out drinkers; lone drifters passing through, and drifters who have settled here and become locals within a year. There are hipsters into aliens, European families touring the States, Japanese students who think they see ghosts, and uniformed military personnel on a break from *up there* at the base. There are retired RV travelers—they're stopping here on their way to Roswell, New Mexico (the other major American UFO tourist site), or to tour petroglyphs through the Southwest as evidence of alien visits to ancient Native Americans.

There are those solitary guys who, everyone knows, have a job *up there* in some working-class capacity at Area 51 but who can't talk about it; they'd go to prison if they mentioned where they were employed. *Ten years in Leavenworth if you talk*, people quietly say. Maybe they spend their days *up there* fixing the plumbing or driving a van, who knew? You could talk all day about what secret plots the government was hatching up there, or about the UFO smuggled in and sitting below layers of red earth. But everyone just knew not to ask too much about what anyone sitting in the café really did, in ordinary time with their own hands, to earn a regular paycheck in that same place. The everyday forbidden knowledge of work at the base was a different kind of secret than the hidden alien bodies or the secret UFO, but it was stitched from the same threads in a partial imaginary of hidden power.

Tourists come here to drive the dirt road through desert ranchland and witness the signs at the perimeter of the secret base: *No Trespassing, No Photography, Deadly Force Authorized.* You can pick up parts of detonated bombs, bits of military debris, scattered among the Joshua trees. Some people use the parts to decorate their trailers. Or you can drive out to the "black mailbox" that belongs to a local rancher—it's said to be the best place to spot *weird stuff* in the sky. (The mailbox had been painted white for years now, to try to elude the tourists, but everyone still called it the black mailbox anyway.) You park and gather around the mailbox on brilliant black midnights and wait to see stars turn into lights that begin to spin and twirl and streak across the sky. Other stars remain stars and hang all the way to the ground. In the deep night sky, a glow on the horizon looks like a huge distant wildfire or a supernatural gleam, but is actually Las Vegas some hundred miles south. In this vast, palpable night you see flares that just disappear, rockets that curve in glorious arcs, orange orbs that float over your head and come down toward you and then shoot off, lights that do right-degree angles at high speeds, three lights in the sky that converge into two, then into one, until the one just disappears. Some of them hovered, split, and made impossible moves. Maybe they were UFOs.

Wayne and Billy are drinking beers after their shift working in the café. They've spent all day washing dishes and flipping burgers. Now here they are, gazing at the stars that seem to pulse across the sky, at the big moon, and the darkness that presses down on your body like a soft, heavy lid. Wayne has lived out here all his life. He's an air force son, and he does the odd jobs that come his way. Billy's moved out for a while after an itinerant path of cities; he's local now too because he's not a tourist. All of a sudden, the local habit of smirking, a bit, over the UFO tourists' high-pitched enthusiasm seems to melt away. Billy and Wayne are reeling and spinning with awe and drunken exuberance, heads tilted back, arms up, glorying over the stars and their own imaginations that fill the open space, exclaiming that they see eternity out here, infinity, UFOs, galaxies, time, all of it in the sky.

Who knows if the moving, arcing, and disappearing lights in the sky are UFOs, or fantastic secret military aircraft? It didn't much matter to many of the watchers. The lights were mysterious and uncanny, whatever their origin. Ricky came out here from his home on the West Coast for months at a time. He just wanted to drive around and *see cool stuff.* He says: I don't really care where the stuff comes from. The stuff they make *up there* is weird enough for me. Maybe it's a really, really new kind of plane and it can do these incredible things. And I just feel like, here I am, on the *cutting edge.* I am seeing things that in twenty years might be common. But right now they're only *here.* And it's just so cool to be able to see them.

I don't really think those lights are UFOs, Ricky muses another time. But, well, where the technology *came* from—that's a different question. *Where did **they** learn how to make that technology?* It doesn't seem to be from this world, does it?

Some say the government hired reverse engineers—that's what the Nazis did, too. Those reverse engineers work for *them.* They dismantled that UFO piece by piece to find out how it worked. And this is how they actually invented the integrated circuit, I had often heard—*we couldn't have done that alone* (see the confessional account by Corso 1998). Some say what those scientists took apart were the crashed extraterrestrial bodies, examining their exotic organs and strange blood. That's what the alien autopsy showed on Fox TV in 1995. *They* captured wounded extraterrestrials after the Roswell crash, wanted to see what was inside them.[1] That's what the aliens do to *us*. They take us apart. To them we are *nothing*, doesn't matter if you yell, scream, or try to fight, they just use your body to get what they need, just like they do to the planet itself. Bleeding nature dry.

And when tourists came up to the cash register to pay for their meal, Pat would sometimes let them know: I heard they saw something *up there* just last night. You go on out to the Black Mailbox— (well it's painted white now)—and that's where you'll see them. This map is thirty cents and that'll show you where to go. If you go at night though, you got to drive slow not to hit a cow. You know, this is open range.

Here we remain in the densely narrativized, entextualized West of John Bourke. But we're at another point in its history: the end of the twentieth century. The tourists are coming here for UFOs now, not for Daniel Boone. Everyone knows the grandeur of the pioneer myth is cracking a bit, losing its monolithic status in light of changing American and global political metanarratives of encounter. The kids' school books are ambivalent, the movies show ironic takes on the myth. Yet all those old memories of colonization, conversion, and genocide linger on, scattered in the old pioneer stories that remain in the desert, close enough to touch. Grandparents who are from this area like to tell you proudly of their own grandparents coming across the plains in the covered wagon, stories they heard early and often enough so that the images entered the nuclei of their cells. *My great-grandfather used a covered team to haul freight to the mines. Fought Indians on the way too.* But those who moved here more recently from back east have similar images and stories dreamed into their cells, too. They hold on tight as it begins to slip.

## Ordinary Marks and Monstrous Mutilations

*Cut 1*

It takes six men to brand the cattle. Harry explains it at the table in the café. One of you on a horse with nine inches of lariat, and you rope the calf and get it down, tie it, two men laying atop of it while another man *brands it* and *cuts it* (neuters it). You inoculate it then too; takes less than one minute. Then the calf is up and running again. You keep three branding irons in the fire at the same time, so one of them is always red hot for the next calf.

Harry and Pete work these big jobs together. They know this land as well as anyone can know land. Out of their nine siblings, only one went east for good.

One day, inside Harry and his wife Joan's sweetly decorated, tidy mobile home, Harry illustrates the shape of his cattle brand with a finger tracing in some cornmeal scattered on a counter. Like a lot of things, branding is a fading art. *Back east they don't know how to brand, anymore. Just tag the cow's ear. That's all.*

That brand on the body of the cow marks the way things were supposed to be done, in a dreamtime before things got out of whack. It was *before*, a time of pride and tradition. That cattle brand done right shows an order of things. What's fading is the sign of a ranchman's dominion over the animal, his ownership cut into it with his knowledge and skill.

The ordinary brand on the body of the cow is the way it was supposed to be. But the animal can be marked *out here* by alien forces too. Sitting in the café on another day, Harry listens while some folks are talking about how *they*—the government, or the aliens or both, just the unknown ever-present *they*—also cut cattle. *They* brand those cows with the mark of the uncanny. I'm wiping down the tables but hearing this talk and I sit down to join them now. I've heard this kind of story often in Hillview before I came out to Nevada—uncanny cattle mutilation is a well-known mystery. *They*—whoever they might be— cut the animals down the middle with a perfect edge, and suck the blood and organs out. Some people say it's coyotes and vultures doing this. *Yeah right*, I heard in Texas and Nevada both. No way it can be coyotes and vultures with a cut that clean.

Human bodies have been found that way too, some say. Cut so clean it had to be done by a laser.

*Cuts: 2*

At the bar one night, Randall talks with Earnest and Harry and me about the uncanny cattle mutilations. *They'd* screwed Ernest over; his health was a wreck since his time in the military. And so nothing *they* did surprised him anymore.

I asked if cattle mutilations were still going on around here. And Randall told this story:

Former senator . . . had a prize BULL
Mutilated within fifty yards of his office.
This one lady,
She had a cattle ranch,
And a prize cow,
(I think it was a cow)
It was *mutilated.*
So they just drug it off
To a remote area.
Well the *coyotes* wouldn't bother it.[2]
The *varmints* wouldn't bother it,
YOU know.
So uh, a couple years later, I think she said,
She was ridin out in that vicinity,
So she just rode by where this cow
Had been *drug* to this place, you know.
And she said of course the top part of it, the skin,
Was all dried out.
But through the head she could see part of the JAW
Where the jaw was removed.
Whatever—mutilated.
And you could see *through* the top part of the head,
The flesh on the lower side, next to the ground,
Looked like it was FRESH KILLED,
And it had been laying' there for two years.
Susan: *Woah!*
Randall: And like I say—the varmints in the desert,
They didn't bother it.
You know, coyotes are scavengers.
They'll eat anything.
Earnest: YUP. Human being or anything else they can get out
    there!
Randall: They'll eat anything—
Earnest: yeah—
Randall:—*but they didn't bother this carcass.*
I heard every one of them [mutilated carcasses]
will you know just LAY there for a long time,
Before it goes back to nature.
Everything else, you know, just rots immediately.
For some reason, *they don't.*

Susan: Well—what do you think it is? *Doing* it?
Randall: It's anybody's guess. I don't believe it's Satan,
I don't believe it's that.
Susan: Yeah, that seems un*like*ly.
Randall: And the precision
of the incision
of these things that are mutilated,
It's as though, you know,
It's a cookie cutter *design*,
you know.
It's not just something that's haphazard.
Or not ragged like an animal bite
Or somethin like that.
So what it is, and *why* it occurs, I don't know . . .
Earnest: We got a book out there in the trailer about it . . .
There was one [mutilated carcass] lying right on the side of the
    road.
And they said it looked like it'd *just been killed*.
[In other words, it never rotted.]
Everything I've ever read, every one of those is EXACTLY
    ALIKE.
Cookie cutter.
The cuts are just absolute, total perfect.

What can you say about the power doing these uncanny mutilations?

There is something here that resonates. It is like what you already
know. You see the carcass but never the killing; for it is secret, yet it
leaves its remainders right in your face, right up next to the road where
you'll find evidence, the trace of its presence. This makes sense; this is
what power feels like. In the many small cuts of everyday life you see
the effects of power, but you don't see the workings of an invisible
hand.

But this power is unnatural. It grossly disrupts the order of things.
It scares off the scavenger varmints, which in God's approved natural
cycle helps dead bodies return to the earth. The imperfect, ragged tear
made by an animal's teeth in the natural world is replaced by the chill-
ing perfection of a clinical, surgical cut.

This dead carcass is too dead. Instead of moving through the process of life and death and decay, the mutilated carcass seems forever to

have been JUST KILLED. Its remains stay horribly on view. The uncannily mutilated bodies are stuck forever in the moment of their injury like an unresolved trauma. *They* mutilate our faith that a wound will change in time.

Why else would the word *mutilated* always denote these perfectly alien deaths, not the raggedly torn-up carcass that the coyotes get to? A torn-up body is natural, but here is what has been mutilated: the unquestioned right of the body to the progress, resolution, and absorption of its own trauma. The mutilated body is reduced to *a cookie cutter* form, an inanimate product, for some medicalized, high-tech inscrutable power. Animals and humans fall on the same side in light of its alien gaze.

You know how they say time heals all wounds. But the thing is, Randall says: with this stuff, some of 'em just don't go back to nature for a long, long time. Just sits there, you know. Mutilated by unseen powers.

*Repair*

Sometimes the idea of the American West becomes a metonym for the past itself. It can be fantastically infused into narratives of disaster and survival. Then the threat of ruin emanates from an uncontrolled technological future realm, and a hypernatural western past is the only chance of redemption. Gloria lives by herself with her many animals way up in the hills, on a pioneer compound she'd constructed from wood and wire. Handmade wooden signs warn off trespassers. She drinks water from the trickling creeks on the ground, and laughs off the idea that it might be tainted by radiation. The animals are everywhere on her place, chickens, goats, donkeys, and dogs. Every once in a while she comes into town with her truck full of dogs, and her personality is so big it fills up the café. Her face is brown and lined, and she laughs and talks, full of a huge, eccentric confidence. Up on her compound, when I visit, she strides across her land, talking to and yelling at the animals. She wants to live like people did *back then*, she says; she wants to live in nature. She gives me lunch outside, cooking over a small burner as we sit on little tree stumps. But when it's cold out, we sit inside, in her small house filled with everything she needs to survive. And outside, faded boards hang with the inadvertent beauty of old metal implements and tools. Things to use.

When the threatening hum of Y2K was in the air, Gloria bought mules. She didn't trust what was going to happen when the cities emptied out. She explained: The fools who depend on computers don't know how to survive in the natural world, but she was not going to let them stop her. The fools will need gas for their cars and they'll be stranded on the sides of the road, paying for what they've let go. Gloria ordered leather harnesses for the mules, and an old-timey covered wagon, from a catalog. Then she hired a former Hollywood stunt man trainer—a relative of a worker in the café—to come out to Nevada from California, and teach her to drive the covered wagon. He was a patient teacher, showing her how to talk to the mules, and how to get them to walk and pull the wagon behind them.

I watched one day while she fed her animals and picked up wood from the ground to burn. She said she'd always be able to survive, the way folks did *back then*.

That same fall, a married couple came through Rachel in pioneer clothes. They were a stern-looking pair driving their own covered wagon across the deserts of the Southwest. They said they were done with the modern world. The seemed to stay in pioneer character all the time you talked with them, responding laconically and briefly. Or maybe that's just the way they were. In any case, like Gloria they said they knew that *when things got bad* they'd be able to live. Now they earned just enough to scrape by, getting the bit of money you needed to live in this world: they parked their wagon on the side of the rural road and allowed themselves to be photographed for a few dollars a shot.

One day, a different married couple from up in northern Nevada stopped in at Rachel, and began to talk at the bar in bitter tones. They said the air force had dropped "chaff" (small metallic particles dumped from the sky by military aircraft to distract radar-guided missiles) over everything on their property, and no one knows what it does to you; *we're* their *guinea pigs*, the husband and wife both said. But worse than the potential damage to their bodies, they said, sonic booms from the air force base nearby cracked their foundation.

It was a place that couldn't be replaced. The government was stealing our air space. Here the sky itself becomes nostalgic as land, usurped and plundered by trespassers, by military booms messing up the clear western air with sonic "graffiti." But it should be yours, as everyone nodded sympathetically at the bar—the way it used to be.

What your air space is, [said the wife],
is the very air you breathe is your air space.

You know it's just like when you buy a piece of property
it's yours to the center of the earth.
It's yours to the infinite, is what it should be.
That's the way it used to be . . .
As long as they do no damage
you wouldn't mind somebody walking across your property . . .
but when they devalue your property—
—Then they're trespassing, interrupted the husband,
—and constantly damaging your property, continued the wife,
they come in and do GRAFFITI all over,
then they're damaging your property . . .
That's what they do us.
They blow out our windows,
knock our trailers off foundations,
they crack our foundation on our building . . .
Some of it's irreparable.
It's an old building; an old historic building.
Over to the stage stop.
Some things you can never replace.
You can never repair.
You can't repair history.
Some things are not tangible money-wise.
You know.
Some of the antiques
and some of the old bottles and stuff like that they broke,
they're irreplaceable.
They could give ya a monetary,
they could say, well, you go to a bottle shop
and buy one like that for ten dollars.
But you'll never find another bottle like that.
So what is that bottle worth?
You know, it's not that.
It's part of our Nevada history. It's part of our culture.
These things are not compensatable.
They say they compensate us.
For the damage they done.
But they don't.

They only partially compensate you.
They only replace the broken window;

or replace a part of a structure—
when you take old antique wood and replace it with new wood
    then what is the value?
And that—that's not reparable. I don't think they can fix that.
—We don't really want to be compensated, said the husband.
We want to be left alone.
That's why we live out in the middle of nowhere.
For the peace and tranquility.
The knowledge that we are free people, out in the middle of
    nowhere.
—Are you native Nevadans? I asked.
—No, said the wife, we're actually California transplants.
We own a café mini-mart.
[She takes out a picture of it.]
The Pony Express stopped here.

As the husband says, it's the "knowledge" of living in a western "nowhere" that makes a texted metanowhere into the most intensely imagined somewhere. There is the history dreamed in California thirty years ago; the auratic objects—the old bottle, the empty space—bulging to contain that dream's "value." There is the magic of the living dead, as ordinary as the "western" looking wooden walls of a mini-mart, but still extraordinary, charged with the master narrative of the frontier past.

And yet, inhabited so fully, attended to so closely, this same master narrative begins to loom strange. Its own effects are heightened, intensified, through a concrete performance. Its own naturalizations begin to give way, like a photograph enlarged and reproduced until it starts to look surreal.

The imaginary of power is contradictory and complex. The air force that borders Rachel commands respect as an ordinary institution, a source of employment and everyday patriotism. But this iteration of the ordinary military is a different character in a different story from that of the government and the *powers that be*. Although Joe chimed in and echoed the couple from northern Nevada (*yeah we are their guinea pigs, that is right*), Joe in fact loved the sonic booms around his parts. Several times a day the sonic booms shock the stillness, then let silence rush back to fill the void. In Rachel, when one man made a complaint that the booms cracked his trailer, others in the town signed a petition in "rebuttal . . . [to] a disgruntled Rachel resident":

*Please don't mistake that boom for a disturbance . . . It's the sound of freedom.*

There is always the excitement of a power that defines and incorporates its partial observers. And the uncanny allure of destruction.

There are more everyday versions of this lived story about the pioneer past and its capacity for redemption. Pat and Joe said they were pioneers, too; they still worked twelve-hour days up here, never complaining, on their feet for hours—in some ways no different from when Pat's mother chopped wood to keep her kids from starving and freezing. And after a whole day of café work, Pat might start her canning, filling the kitchen sink with peaches and jars, in a proud habit of surviving that metamorphosed slightly, in the rural West, into the apocalyptic survivalist habit of storing food. Here it isn't strange to store quantities of food. Yes, it feels good to know we did that ourselves, Joe would say, surveying the homely mess in the sink below cabinets stocked with rows of store-bought canned beans, on sale at the Vegas Price Chopper.

Work and independence. Those were key. It was important to be able to help out your neighbor, and to be able to help yourself. Dorothy was an elderly woman who had come out here live with her middle-aged daughter. If you asked her what she thought about the UFOs, she politely said, "Well, to each his own." She was quiet and sharp, and her own life was an unmarked story of pioneer survival. Only when you asked, she would tell about getting married in her teens and having six children, "four living." Her story of moving west as a younger woman was an old one with deep grooves. The husband went first to look for work, and she followed later with the children, but then she found out it was his brother who had sent the bus ticket. *Didn't you want us to come?* Hell no, he said—he was having too much fun.

She had to stand on her own two feet to support those kids and she did. After their divorce, she was working full-time in a fast-food restaurant and had four part-time jobs. And she got so tired, she went down to the welfare office to ask for "some help"; she only wanted:

The equivalent of two days' pay. For three months.
And I would pay it back to the state.
But I needed some time to rest.

But she found the state would not help her maintain her independence, would not give her the bit of rest she needed so she could carry on. She gave a pointed look as she commented on that irony:

> If I would quit my job,
> they would take care of me and my family,
> for life.
> I told em:
> *When I drop dead feed my family.*

She was used to working hard and she didn't want them to take that away. She described the rural Midwestern winters before moving west, where her husband had been a blacksmith with seasonal work; and they would get so cold and be so penniless that he'd have to go down to the coal yard for a gunnysack of coal, "and I got so worried I was sick." She would cook potatoes and corn on the small heating stove, and they would do all right. And she was sure of her competence to survive:

> We didn't have but a third of the five-gallon bucket full of coal.
> To keep the house warm or keep the fire going.
> So I ordered the half ton of coal
> and the dray brought it out as far as the driveway . . .
> Because it was a six-foot deep drift
> and he couldn't get the horses and dray through it.
> I says, dump it in the ditch.
> I tied an apple box on the kids' sled
> And hauled that coal back an apple box at a time
> And put it in the coal shed.
> And kept the fire going day and night
> And there was ice inside the house, on the windows.
> I put the kids to bed that night with their snowsuits on and
>     their overshoes
> With hot rocks wrapped in newspapers at their feet.
> And covered up good.
> I had strung blankets around the stove,
> the potbelly stove,
> And had the double bed for the kids and the cot for me.
> And put them to bed there.
> There was three or four of em at that time,

Anyway, they didn't catch a cold or anything. And the house
    never got warm.
Got up to about 30 [degrees]
a few feet away from the stove.
But they never got cold or sick.
You do a lot of things if you have to.
But after my divorce
I had enough to keep us going.
And I didn't spend it on things we didn't need.
And it was just fine.


Stories of freedom and independence weave into the fabric of who
you are, standing up to a government that tries to worm in and pull
you down. They try to make you weak by refusing to help in the way
that would work with your own fierce abilities. Instead they try to
usurp your autonomy with a cunning gentle force, to chip away at the
pride you rightly have in all you could do without them. That's what
they were still doing, *up there*, taking over people's bodies, and making
their evil deals with unworldly powers that be.

Stepping into the café, other themes come to the foreground, other
ways to figure the real. In the constant interplay of everyday life and its
uncanny parallels, you can witness and feel how they coproduce each
other's dreams.

"The military base? It don't bother me," says Harry. "It don't bother
the cows. Don't make them stampede, they get used to it, the planes
come down real close over their heads and they don't pay it no mind.
The horses—well, they do get spooked."

What is it that spooks the horses?

"I don't think it's UFOs," says Harry. "Maybe later it will be; but
not now."

His wife Joan says, "I do think it's UFOs. My former husband and I
we liked to travel. Once, we went to Utah. Well, driving on the road
they made everyone pull over, and there was a UFO on the back of a
military vehicle. A big flying saucer; it was a UFO. This whole thing
has been going on for hundreds and hundreds of years. The UFOs went
to South America, and did those petroglyphs."

I was surprised to hear her so opinionated—she was usually defer-
ential to her husband. Before she moved out here and married him,

Joan lived in another state, worked in the air force development indus-try. She lived on a farm, but worked on the edge of high tech.

But she is animated as she says, "I have seen some *weird things* out here. How about that plane the color of the sky?"

Harry nods, agreeing. "It didn't make noise. I saw its shadow. Went right overhead but you can't see it. Only way you know to look up is cause it throws a shadow. That's all you see, its shadow."

Joan chimes in, "You only see a shadow. That's the only way you know it's there, by the shadow on the ground."

Harry repeats, "Only by the shadow." But then he looks at her with a small shift. He shakes off the uncanny.

"It's just planes, made in America. Don't bother me that they have secrets. They need to have secrets to protect the people of the country. Those are airplanes, not UFOs."

I say to Harry, "I have a feeling you only believe in what you see with your own eyes."

He soberly nods. "That's right."

It isn't the military that bothers him. But the government should keep its nose out of his business. Its long arm impedes you, blocking open range like a sudden fence in the middle of his way.

Though sometimes, you can't see what you're bumping into. All you see is its effect on the ground. A *something* that gives you a faint sudden shiver, though when you look up to see what has happened nothing is there. You don't see the power that maybe protects or maybe violates you, that incorporates you into its own invisible shape. But there it is anyway, seen in its effects on the ground, the darkness it casts, and the shiver. Its shadow.


## Invisible Powers

Even after the military's grudging admission in the mid-1990s that an experimental military base the size of Connecticut did, perhaps, not *not* occupy central Nevada, the military kept observers away (see Jacobsen 2011). Patrolling the unmarked borders in white Cherokee Jeeps, Area 51 guards arrested blundering hikers, Green-peace activists, and constitutionalist activists alike. (Only in the summer of 2013 did the CIA finally acknowledge, officially, that Area 51 does in fact exist.) Everyone knew the truth for decades before the official word was released. At the guard posts, signs warned you that deadly force is authorized for stepping onto a non-existent place.

These encounters with the borders of power generate both rumor and silence. In Rachel, people talked about how *they* forced down a small plane that meandered accidentally into the forbidden air space known as Dreamland. A crew of military guys dragged the lost pilot from his plane and injected him with something that just knocked him right out. Last thing that poor guy saw was a military man kneeling on top of him, with a huge, hypodermic needle. After *they* figured out that he was a small-time pilot with a bad sense of direction and not a spy, they dumped him at the border of the base. He lost time, like Travis Walton.

Frank, a dignified, intelligent retired miner, a lifelong rural westerner who paid little attention to Area 51, told of going hunting for chuckers (partridges) in the mountains and inadvertently getting too close to the border. Seven helicopters *buzzed him*, circling in tighter and tighter, lower and lower, though they are not supposed to fly down on civilians like that.

Frank got out of his pickup. The military guys said they were protecting him: *There's live ordinance around here*, they told him. Oh right, he said with a sarcastic twinkle, they had to make sure he was safe with all that live ordinance around.

Then they said they had to be careful because they have to watch out for Greenpeace. (*Did I look like Greenpeace? In a tiny, canary-yellow pickup?*) They were, he said, very rude, and he—clearly not someone to be taken for a tourist or a Greenpeace rabble-rouser—told them they'd better *put up a post* in that area to warn folks if there was live ordinance around. They did it, too. They put up a post. But just telling this story made him begin to speak stiffly with memory of the insult. *I would not bother them up there*, he said, *and anyone that does is just stupid.*

Sometimes you would see the guards in their white Cherokees. They were just men sitting in a Jeep with the doors wide open in the hot Nevada sun, blaring their radios. It was, on one level, just another tedious job around here; *yeah they used to be employed by Wackenhut, now it's uh, something else*, some other contractor who hired in a hard-bitten place where it was not easy to get a job. The border guards looked young and bored.

And Frank had another story about them too. Once, he was trapping up there with his two granddaughters. Coyote and wildcat. They set traps right next to the border of the base and went on home. And no one bothered them, even when they went right up next to the border. But the next day, they were a whole *mile* away from the border, and all of a sudden those guards in white Cherokees came speeding over the bumpy road with their warning lights flashing. Making a big display of Frank getting too close, when really this time he was pretty far away from the forbidden line. So Frank and the little girls talked to the young fellas who pulled them over.

"Well," said Frank, "I was a lot *closer* [to the border] yesterday. I was right next to the sensor, and you *knew* I was here then. Why didn't you stop me then?" "Oh, well, you know," said the guards. "Live ordinance around here," they said, shrugging. (Frank smiles a piercing smile that hints, *Live ordinance, yeah—that's what they always say*.) Today, Frank thought, it seemed they were just bored, sitting around in their Jeeps; they were bored young fellows and felt like using their flashing lights, just felt like having an encounter. These guards embodied the huge, secret power; they could choose to remain invisible, or to force encounters whenever they arbitrarily wished to reveal the material force behind its pervasive, invisible surveillance.

Then as they stood there, in deference to the representatives of secret power, Frank's little granddaughter tugged his leg, whispering and pointing to the guard's Cherokee.

"What's she saying?" asked the guard.

"That you guys have a flat tire," Frank replied.

The same year as Pat's Nevada tourism award, *Popular Mechanics* published a widely read story asserting that all covert military operations had ceased at Area 51 and been moved to a new site in the Utah desert. But Rachel people mostly refuted the magazine's claim. The reporter's story, they said, was attention-grabbing (well that's what sells magazines) but wrong. (The *X-Files* got it wrong too. They shot an episode that was supposed to be in Rachel—in the café, we sent them souvenirs to use as props—but their set didn't look a thing like Rachel.) Local people said the *Popular Mechanics* reporter actually drove up the wrong unmarked dirt rancher's road, and so he saw none of the warning signs or checkpoints that famously signal the beginning of forbidden land. And so, people shrugged (with their humorously deadpan way of conveying just how silly he was), he *just went home*. Didn't even *stay* here long enough to see the weird lights with unnatural movements that appear regularly over the town at night. You can see them all the time. Well just look up, and there they are.

Still, on the other hand, maybe it wouldn't be surprising to anyone here if UFO talk was in fact moving on, following the constant elusive *elsewhere* constructed in all uncanny conspiracy discourse, with its restless centers that do not hold. Nor would anyone be surprised if it was all just plain closing down, the way so many things did in the rural West; that's what happened around here, to mines, jobs, and towns. And as for bringing lots of revenue into the county, it hadn't really panned out anyway. At a county meeting held at the café one night to discuss fixing county roads and details of the upcoming sheriff election, someone called out, *Only Rachel gets anything from UFOs around here.* UFOs had brought tourist money to a couple of businesses, but the other towns hadn't seen it, they implied. And there was a sense that the peak of tourism and fame might have coincided with the intimation of its own inevitable obsolescence in Rachel.

## Missive from Washington

The federal government—ambiguously mythologized in the nineteenth-century West as omnipotent in genocidal campaigns and invisible in the daily anarchies of a "Wild West"—still retains that magic duality here. The imagination of government here is both pervasive and shrouded.

In a desert café, surrounded by pictures of UFOs, a teenage kid plays pool for hours with a middle-aged friend who's had a few too many. But the kid is trying to straighten out so he'll have a chance to get out of nowhere by joining up with the army's good deal. If he can get into the military, he'll be able to go somewhere. He will learn a skill and some discipline, and return as a man, get a good job and pay child support for his baby living in another town. He might shine, like another boy who left the desert and went to West Point. The military offers that familiar conversion narrative.

But alongside the ordinary hope of a military career for a boy at a crossroads in a rural place, there is the absent omnipotence of military power. Here in this place where invisible planes are stealthily made, where nuclear bombs were tested in the sky and underground, some say the poison is still here and still emerging and that it has riddled the place with cancer. Others disagree; when Gloria drinks her water off the ground she says this is the deep rural countryside with the freshest air and water you could ask for. A man in his sixties remembers without rancor how the atomic test blasts blew windows out of his boy-hood home in northern Arizona, ninety miles away from the center of the explosion in Nevada. Another recalls seeing the sky flash while he rode his horse across the spare subtleties of this land he probably knew better than the planes of his own body. *Didn't bother us any. Didn't hurt us a bit.*

There is excitement in power. The salesman drove out from another state, telling us about all the government secrets he knew; he was equipped with hundreds of dollars of scanners and night-vision goggles. He let some of us peer through them as we hung out at the black mail-box, so we could see the dark desert all in green, the Joshua trees like underwater plants, and the strange little lights emanating in the sky from Dreamland.

But omnipotent, invisible *powers that be* emerge darkly when die-hard independent men clench their jaws, thinking of the government that for some incomprehensible reason owns all the ranchland. Across these expanses, the stately pace of your cattle and their low, brass sym-phony heals your need for words. You laid down the miles of pipe un-derground, even into the outer rim of covert military land where you have a special dispensation to chase your cattle, and now water flows here in a hard place. Things are going well. The land is yours in the deepest sense. But *they* don't acknowledge that. The wives get a head-ache when they think of it, while collecting the ostrich eggs (the os-trich business does better in Texas, she hears, better in the South), or weeding the garden, or driving more than a hundred miles to get some medicine from Wal-Mart.

American western continuity, felt to be inextricable from the land, can itself inspire the bitterness of its inevitable loss. It is a loss that echoes with other losses, come and gone before. From here the EPA is entitled, privileged know-it-alls who can steal all this on some whim. They can divert your water, or shut down your well, or try to close the nearest dump—which is already a hundred miles away!—cause some damn endangered *rat* got in it. You can't keep animals out of a dump! Besides, your friend adds in, as you bond over it at the bar, the wild animals *like* dumps—coyotes, wildcats—it's where they go to *get their munchies*. What do *they* know of this in Washington?

Some people in these parts pour themselves into their hard rural work. You improvise a way to fix something in one of its endless variations of wear and tear. There is a tangible, unspoken satisfaction when your improvisation works, because your skill has become un-thinking, and your mind is alive, focused and in synch with your hands. That unspoken satisfaction carries a lot of weight and transforms the ache of physical labor. Its feel of independence seems a part of the place's birthright.

Harry has made everything on his little farm a few miles from Rachel, all wood and metal. He does his outdoor work with a fast, graceful efficiency and, like Frank, he pays no mind to that Area 51 business. But Harry does agree with the neighbors' bitter critique of the powers that be in Washington. Used to be, you could go out and rope a wild jackass. No more. They say it's cruelty to animals. It isn't cruelty to animals, cause the animals *get too thick*. Like the wild horses out here, got too *thick*. They'll just starve. They overgraze the land. People out *here'd* shoot 'em, feed 'em to the pigs. Sell the bones! There is no waste involved. Otherwise you get too many wildcats and coyotes and they starve too. But you can't shoot 'em, anymore.

Over the years, land has been seized in this area of Nevada—by the military, wanting more forbidden miles around the base; you can see on the maps in the Area 51 Research Center—how the places you aren't allowed to go have expanded. Looking at these maps is eerily like looking at historical maps of Indian reservations in this area and seeing the expanding land around their borders over the years.

Centuries of political struggle between the federal and the local, between the urban and the rural, escalated in many ways in the 1970s (see Davis 1997). But for many people in the rural West, details of a political struggle are expressed in a narratively compressed shorthand as you align yourself with the West and the rural, with decades of sagebrush rebellions against federal control of land and urban ideas of what nature ought to be. A wider sense of rip-off gets distilled into a sense of an undifferentiated power that's after your autonomy and the land you inhabit. It's a sense that is in fact bolstered by the complexities of land politics and its sometimes strange alignments. Wildlife is in fact protected on the base; the tanks must stop in their tracks for the endangered desert tortoise (Patten 1997).

A natural cycle has been disrupted by the government. It doesn't seem right. Powers with no connection to this place throw a wrench in the interconnected chains of life and death that make up this land, natural connections that he regards as integral to his livelihood. But they claim to be the advocates of nature, the protectors of the environment. What do *they* know about it—the words *animal cruelty* are disrespectful, given all the care and knowledge with which he keeps the chicken coop so clean, and rigs up a low little spout for the pigs to drink fresh water any time they want, and feeds all the animals natural alfalfa or grain instead of slops; he can sell people down in Flagstaff organic eggs and meat, because they like that. The alfalfa comes from the big farm right in Rachel, whose hay throwers frequent the bar in the café to drink and carouse a bit along with the workers from *up there* at Area 51. Meat you raised yourself is better than store-bought, so he doesn't know if he prefers to sell his pigs or eat the pork himself.

He feeds the runt piglet by hand, kneeling down in his cowboy hat, his stiff shirt tucked neatly into his jeans, his square jaw dignified, silently holding the pink, plastic baby bottle to its tiny mouth.

Harry's goat is good for both her silky alpaca coat, and her milk. He says: *Come on. Come on now*, in a low firm voice, and the pretty little goat trots over, jumps on the wooden milking platform Harry made by hand, and puts her head through a metal loop to get in position for milking. The goat gets herself in place and then checks in with Harry, looking back at him over her shoulder. After Harry milks her he says, I made this stand too wide. I'll make a new one tomorrow. A narrower platform will get him closer to the goat when he milks. He is always improving on the way things work.

In five years Harry and Joan plan to be entirely self-sufficient. They will show people that you can do it. Harry will build a smokehouse for homemade bacon. The first time I had a conversation with Joan, over at Pat's house, she mentioned that in their two years of marriage Harry had *never once tasted store-bought bread*—she bakes it all herself. They've got their dairy products, eggs, chicken, the garden. They have grazing cattle. All they'll need is salt and pepper, and they can go get that kind of thing once a year.

Harry grew up on a farm in the Southwest; but he has moved around and did other kinds of work. Heating and cooling. Up in Reno, get up any time of day or night when they called to fix the air conditioner. He has been a sheet metal worker, and he has worked in a mine. He talks about these jobs with the same balanced pride as he does his ranch and farm work. But he nearly always had animals. After some time in the Midwest he longed to come back to his roots in the West. Because you can go anywhere on open range, and no one's gonna bother you or tell you not to.

Except of course at the base.

But there was one day when I was with Harry in his truck; he waved to the guard at the checkpoint at the forbidden base and then we drove on in, because he had permission to go up a bit and follow his wandering cattle. My breath came fast, driving past the notorious red-and-white signs: Keep Out, Deadly Force Authorized. White sensors that looked like periscopes stuck up among the stunted twists of Joshua trees. Poles topped by silver balls dotted the ground and I craned to see them as we bounced along the dirt road. *Are those the heat sensors?* I asked Harry. People had told me the heat sensors could distinguish between a cow and a deer. One person even said the heat sensors could differentiate between specific animals of the same species, so that a couple of rancher's cows were allowed to roam but others would be driven out. Harry didn't pay attention to the sensors. *That's air force,* he said simply. He was showing me the water lines, where he and his brother had put in all the pipes so the cows could drink up here. He was proud of this, talking fast, in his stoic, concise way. He told me how they'd found the right spots for the water lines, and what kinds of materials they used.

Later on, after we left the military area, we decided to climb up onto the ruins of an old mine on Tempiute Mountain. We ran up the sides. He ran up the steep rocky hill in his cowboy boots as fast as a goat, with his dignified white head, weathered face, upright upper body, and a cigarette dangling from in his mouth. He showed me the old, caving-in tunnel, vestigial tracks that disappeared into nothing, materialized bits of the prospector past. But all of a sudden a man imperiously approached us, seemingly out of nowhere.

*What are you doing here? Get out, you cannot be here,* he said to Harry.

Harry's response was formal and formidably polite. Still the man was overbearing, authoritative, ignoring Harry's dignity and rudely pointing us the way out.

Was the man military or Union Carbide? Was this barren place still in secret use? Was it a mine coming back to life, or was it being surreptitiously maintained by some source of power threatened by our presence? We had no idea. Like Frank, up at the base that time confronted by white Cherokees, Harry's dignity had been insulted. He was an upstanding man. He would not knowingly go where he was not supposed to go. He was a professional rancher in a starched shirt and ironed jeans, twice the age of the man who ordered him about with unknown forces backing his authority. Harry was not to be taken for a vagrant, a lowlife, a radical, or a troublemaker.

We got back in his pickup. *He shouldn't have talked that way. We weren't doing nothing wrong.* He was contained and polite as ever, but all the way home his jaw was set tight, and he was quiet. Quietly burning.

At home his wife says: "The ones back east don't know anything about it here, or why we do the way we do, but the ones back east are the ones who make the rules."

Things around here were changing. Harry did not analyze it much; he worked, and fixed things, and had deep knowledge of what he did. But asked about what was making things change out here, he said, "The environmentalists."

For the rational, no-nonsense rancher, and for the area's fabulous conspiracy theorists alike, *environmentalism* was a word with a dark, strange aura. The EPA was an agency that tried to control policy on the open range. Its policies viewed the land as public in many ways, required to expand its use beyond grazing into such public uses as national parks. Conservative constituencies in the West traditionally clashed with both the EPA and the BLM for economic reasons. But in story, for some people who had no direct economic interest in the potential development of land, those acronyms also had become a kind of fantastically demonic emblem of the powers that be and its dominion over land; it was an enemy of the individual, and a right arm of the New World Order that would subsume you in its wake. People often talked about the EPA, not mentioning specific policies but letting the sound of the initials resonate with an implicit, amorphously sinister implication.


## Stolen Land

Randall and Earnest were at the bar again another day, talking together about the powers that be. And Randall said, "Constitutionally they [the government] can't own any land in this United States except a ten-mile strip of land called Washington, DC. But somehow they rob the people of the land. And thereby the people can't come out here and use the land as they see FIT. They're even trying to put the ranchers out of business. They're saving this land for—for—WHATEVER."

> Susan: (thinking he meant military seizures of land, at the
> base, not the EPA) You mean like nuclear experiments?

Randall: I think it's more closely related to the New World Order. The UN!
You know this so-called EPA
is nothing but a communist plan
to eliminate the people from the land.
Of course this is my opinion, from what I have read.
This American heritage thing!
This rivers act!
If they get this into effect, the government will control the watershed.
They're destroying our country right before our eyes.
Earnest: It's called PEOPLE CONTROL.
Randall: It's called PEOPLE CONTROL. That's illegal.
Earnest: You can't even go walk a trail—without paying the government—you gotta go get a TICKET. To walk a TRAIL.
[He says the word "ticket" in disgust.]
They have made it impossible for you or I
to stake a CLAIM.
But there are several gold and silver companies from England.
*They have no restrictions whatsoever.*

This land was still being fought for. Nature was still being taken captive. Something alien coming from the federal government was staking out a land claim, imperiously asserting its right to decide what was best for the land and the people who lived on it, *taking away* how they had lived. Buying a ticket from the government to "walk a trail" showed how it was not, in fact, a free public national space—it belonged to *them*. And *they* did not represent Earnest. This was the place where you should be able to stake a claim like the old-timers; it used to be a kind of jackpot in the mountains north of Vegas. But now you could not try your luck with the land; only other players in a global game were allowed. It had become big-time, and *they* had gotten it all for themselves.

Here an anti-corporate discourse merges with a conservative one (against land protection) that often serves corporate interests. But that is not the point of this conversation; the point is the felt sense of an amorphous alien power, grabbing things up, stealing your pride away, and thinking *they* know the rules of nature.

The counternarrative of federal protection has an uncanny resonance, the sense of a terrible thing that you just know in your bones to be true. It has the impact of a chime with other stories of this land's colonization by the federal government—not just the histories of federal and local struggles, but also the unfinished legacy of settlement and missionization, haunting the landscape with a shifting, unstable point of view. Who were the natives here? Who was going to take away their land, their way of life? The question, lurking in the background, could summon ghosts.

"You can almost imagine an old chief sitting up there," said Edith, the elderly airforce widow, gazing up at the cliff.

Who lived here, before?

"I don't know," she muses, "maybe the Sioux."

"Had a book about it one time, had a blue cover," offers John.

Where are they now?

Nick was a local cowboy who one day gave me an arrowhead he'd found in the desert. I put it in a little plastic case from a gumball machine, so it wouldn't break. I didn't know if it was really an arrowhead, but I knew people liked to find them, collect them. Some people put them up in framed arrangements on their trailer walls.

But talking with Nick, I thought even the cowboy in the cowboy-and-Indian story feels himself to be inside the narrative's denouement.

An overweight tourist in a big flowered hat—a loud imposing presence—pushed open the café door and seized the air in the room. She interrupted Nick in the middle of his sentence about roping.

WHERE'S THE UFO? she demanded. IS THERE A UFO HERE TODAY?

A bit later Nick ruefully said: We [cowboys] are dinosaurs.

## Ordinary Brands: Cuts 3

I come walking up to the café one afternoon and there's Nate pacing in front.

"Hey—look at this," he says.

Nate holds up a big dead swaying rattlesnake, which he grips by the neck. I bend to see. Its face fills the visual field between us with an ordinary alienness—its pointed head, its blank obsidian eyes.

"Roadkill," Nate says. "I'm gonna take it and throw it on the grill. You ever eat snake? It's good. Well, I was here waitin' for you to show it to you."

I agree to come over later and try it with them.

But he's been waiting for a different reason. Not so much because

I'll enjoy the meat but because, he explains, "Thought you'd want to take a picture of it." He guesses rightly that as a New Yorker, I would find the snake interesting.

"Thanks," I say. I go inside and get my camera, and come back to where he is waiting.

Nate holds the snake up for my camera. This is his sign of his place, consciously performed for the city outsider. The rattlesnake, the meta-icon of rugged dangerous desert, entextualizes Nate now. He is holding it up like a fisherman with a big barracuda. In this image familiar to us both, he is a desert guy in a cowboy hat and a lip-dangling Marlboro, a guy who throws a rattlesnake on the grill. He's still a teenager, but he is a father to a baby, and needs to find ways to earn money and be a man. He does manual labor when there's work; maybe he'll join the military. He clowns and performs his meta-cowboy look, a self-consciously sultry grin; I laugh and snap the picture.

I try to imagine Nate at the moment he was finding the snake on the empty road. From far away, through his dirty windshield, he and his young friends can spot glints and shadings that mark a change in the landscape, things that are invisible to me until pointed out and then to me they still look as small and nondescript as a seed. To me, Nate's discerning eye is an incredible skill, but to him it's normal, nothing. As we drive bumping and fast along a dry creek bed he sees a tiny glitter and realizes that it is a beer can, and by the colors that mark its brand, he knows who has been by here since the last time he drove the creek bed, and yup, that someone *must* have done the notorious bit of mischief that everyone had been speculating about.

I think of him speeding as usual and noticing a slight flash in the dirt as sun hit the snakeskin, and then bumping over in his truck to see what it might be, crouching down in the dust, smiling when he sees the snake's still good and whole. I wonder if all this is background in his own mentally developing picture of himself. For holding a rattle-snake is both for my picture and for his own, it figures "authentic rural West" and "Nevada," and so does making use of anything you find in the scarcity of the desert—a mode of survival, a pragmatic bricolage. That's what he signals in his Marlboro Man smile.

Eating roadkill can also figure a different kind of danger in other parts of the United States: of poverty and things "picked up" from the margins of catastrophes. Yet out here, that bleakness doesn't enter the image Nate's performing for me. Instead, he wants to show in a single sign: Things out here are *made use of*, pragmatic and resourceful, clearly and consciously so, something a New Yorker like me would want in a picture. And I do. I snap the camera.

"All right then," he says, nodding courteously.

They don't ever cook it, though. Later that night, Nate comes back to the trailer with just the rattle, a gift for a young local child I am watching. She will want to keep it in a box at her bedside, next to the precious hollowed-out ostrich egg from a nearby ostrich ranch. Ostriches are the gold of the future, some say.

Nate says: "We didn't eat that snake: my cousin said we don't know if it bit itself in that cooler. If you cook it, you burn the poison off. But when they get that scared enough to bite themselves, when they see the truck coming? It makes the meat go bad. Like when you scare a deer before you shoot it, the meat goes bad."

We poke at the cleaned rattle in his palm. When the snake or deer gets too scared the meat goes bad. You eat its fear, and you get sick too. Tainted by adrenaline, the meat must be thrown away.

There it is resonating in so many ordinary moments. Poking that rattle we know that fear becomes a substance with its own effects. Nate and I understand together that trauma seeps outside the moment to stain and alter things when the moment of violence has past. I took another picture of the rattle in his hand.

## CHAPTER 5

# Here Comes a Change

## *At Home in the Weird*

The stories are everywhere, piling up, splitting off, converging. People in the Hillview UFO Experiencers Support Group tell stories constantly. We talk in cars on the way to the meeting (where we are going to tell and listen to stories) and then we tell them on the phone afterward. We tell UFO stories in living rooms and on front porches; in the disinfected radiance of a late-night Shoney's; in chandeliered hotel spaces designed for business conferences but rented for the performance of an abductee's narrated memory.

These are stories about the teller's weird experiences, and metastories about each other's stories. They are also interpretive reworkings of public stories from an always-growing canon of UFO lore. Deeply felt memories are entextualized and intertexutalized with other circulating abduction narratives (Bauman and Briggs 1992). Some narratives are unmarked fragments, seamlessly emerging and vanishing back into bits of conversation. Others are self-consciously artful stories, set up and framed by performance techniques such as "Now I'm going to tell you what happened to me." Some stories are embellished with illustrations. One member brings in his hand-drawn cartoons of aliens on lined notebook paper, laughing, a little humble; another shows paintings of UFOs propped up against a wall at her home, glowing in reds and yellows, with the backgrounds a mysterious black.

Sometimes people tell about UFOs they have seen or heard of. They tell about saucer-like disks or cigar-shaped hovering objects, or specks of light the size of stars that turn at unnatural ninety-degree angles. They tell of a vast thing low in the sky, composed of multicolored lights that dripped beauty and terror as the watcher's car sped below on the bridge outside Hillview. They tell of looking up and witnessing geometric shapes whose corners are punctuated by pulsing lights that move as a single unit; brilliant floating lights waking them from sleep and then suddenly disappearing; or an amorphous glow, rising over a dark horizon of the memory.

Sometimes people tell of aliens: the clinical little grays with big watchful eyes and doctor tools that everyone talks about these days; or sinister men in black, or the trickster-like Reptilians. There are also presences, faces, unfathomable anxieties, sudden comfort coming from the unknown in bleak moments, and bits of inexplicable, half-remembered song. There are animals glimpsed in the dark of a road, or invisible floods of terror and grace that seem to rain down from some alien source. Then there are the amorphous black shapes that hover over sleeping bodies, invisible forces that press down on your chest, creatures who look like cartoon characters who contacted you as a tiny child, and benevolent "Beings" who silently appear, dressed in white flowing robes (or once, in hiking clothes).

Emmalyn (not her real name), the founder of the Hillview UFO Experiencers Support Group, was a long-sober veteran of Alcoholics Anonymous. She said AA was the only true church of Christ she had found, if one existed, a place where people loved you for who you were. She wanted the same community feeling to grow here. Full acceptance, come as you are. She put an ad in the local paper calling for people who'd had possible experiences with UFOs, to meet as a support group in a reserved room at the library. About thirty people showed up the first time.

Emmalyn changed the name of the Hillview group from Alien Abductees Support Group (because that term was too limiting a definition, too exclusive) to a support group for UFO "Experiencers." The word *experiencers* expressed an entire view on the value of experience and expertise. It was a homey phenomenology. It was a way to talk about whatever *the real* might be.

A core of about twelve people remained in the group for years, spanning changing group names and different leaderships, beginning in the early 1990s. They came every week, and then sometimes more than once a week. They hung out at each other's homes, soon marking the group as their main source of sociability by spending Friday and Saturday nights together, having UFO parties on Christmas and New Year's Eve, and sometimes, on summer nights, camping out to search the skies for UFOs.

While the Hillview group was forming, a specific discourse about alien abduction was becoming highly visible and circulating quickly in America. Its narrative strove toward a codified form, creating hegemony from within its wider marginality.[1] Little grays, missing time, clinical experiments on bodies, recovered memory: these were the haunting elements of an increasingly standard abduction narrative. Alien abductees were hypnotized and recovered unnervingly similar hidden memories of clinical violation. Like any genre, the alien abduction narrative became a recognizable form through inclusions and exclusions of material; still it was layered with other genres, saturated with other histories, at once emergent and residual, shot through always with other talk (Bakhtin 1981; Williams 1977).

On one level, the alien abduction genre unconsciously accrued to and resonated with the wider, polysemous genre of captivity narratives about selves, alien others and power. On another level (as I said in chapter 1) alien abduction researchers of the 1980s and 1990s actively distinguished between stories that "fit" the emerging typology, and idiosyncratic accounts that seemed always to hover in the margins with incongruous material. Alien narratives that were too quirky, or that deviated too widely from the increasingly conventionalized story that had come into focus for them, were distractions from that truth. And they were hurting the mission of abductees: to earn mainstream belief (Jacobs 1994). For Budd Hopkins and other similar researchers, the mounting, inexplicable repetitions in these stories were, in short, evidence. Hopkins did not say the little gray aliens were from "outer space," necessarily; but they had to be from somewhere. How could people have such similar memories if something was not really happening, these researchers asked? The strange memories lined up, and the sequences became parallels.

People in Hillview discussed the introduction to Hopkins's widely read mass- market book *Intruders* (which documented his hypnosis-based investigative work with abductees, and showed the repeated pattern of events between various abduction cases); in an analogy often discussed in UFO communities, Hopkins compared the public's skepticism about alien abduction to an earlier generation's inability to accept the magnitude of the Holocaust as it was occurring during World War II. People talked about how Hopkins quoted Judge Felix Frankfurter's response to an eyewitness to the death camps: "[Frankfurter] did not imply that [this witness] had not in any way told the truth, he simply meant that he could not believe him" (Hopkins 1987: xii). Hopkins said that alien abduction accounts were likewise considered fantastic not because they were impossible, but because of our own inability to believe them.

People in the Hillview support group approved of Hopkins's Justice Frankfurter analogy. But they interpreted it more radically: they were open to any abduction memory told in good faith, not just to the dominant type of (often recovered) memory favored by Hopkins and his school of abduction experts. For the Hillview support group, nothing was unbelievable just because it deviated from a standard or codified form, even if that form comprised alien abduction narratives. What made a story real wasn't its iteration of any dominant abduction narrative type, but rather its more subtle iterations, mimeses, and parallelisms—the story's resonance with the everyday containments and captivities you just know from living in the world.

## Tricky Ways of Getting Eggs

Sometimes, abductees in Hillview did tell memories that fit the standard alien abduction form. Christina was stylish and lived in a modern mansion way up in the comfortable hills, a place full of glass and light. Her husband had made his wealth in business, and she focused on making art and on exploring uncanny dimensions of experience. None of it fazed her. Once I was at her home, sitting on her lovely back porch looking over the hills, and we were discussing the conspiracies of black or unmarked helicopters that seemed to weirdly trail UFO experiencers. All of a sudden, a helicopter appeared and began hovering and circling noisily right above her house, practically drowning out our discussion. I could hardly believe the uncanny coincidence; Christina calmly said, "Yes, this is what they do."

At one of our group meetings she told her story, in a similarly calm and graceful way:

> Because I had what I called
> blank time in my day,
> when people said, you know,
> when I was confronted and asked *where did the baby go,*
> *what happened to the fetus,* I couldn't recall.
> I never went to the doctor,
> and nobody ever asked me if I needed help,

or let's go to the doctor,
let's check this out, throughout the whole time.
Never saw anyone [for a prenatal checkup.]
So from beginning to end.
Through hypnosis . . .
I finally got into my subconscious
deep enough to recall what had happened.

And I remember getting up in the middle of the night.
I don't know what woke me
but *something* made me get up.
I walked down the hallway
and where I saw smoke
and I thought there was a fire.
But there was no smoke smell.

When I walked into the living room area,
the whole room was filled with these little lines of vapor,
like the trails of a stick of incense.
And I'm looking around,
and I just have a few seconds in that room
before I was touched on the back of my hip . . .
with something sharp.
At that point it must have been something to put me under.
And I just remember that I was in a prone position after that.
And immobilized.
I remember having my nightgown on,
and my nightgown was lifted
and a syringe-looking thing
with white liquid was put inside me,
it was a great deal of liquid put in there,
a full six inches of white liquid.
And uh, I remember that it burned very much.
And after that my next memory
is standing at the side of my bed,
and then getting into the covers
and (sigh) then waking up in the morning with no memory of
     what had happened
—only that as I sat up
I remembered in the area of my ovaries

I was just burning.

I was really burning.

At that point I WAS pregnant.

Abduction catches you in so many different ways. It conflates the sexual (*and my nightgown was lifted*) with the medical (*and a syringe-looking thing with white liquid was put inside me*), condensing always-latent, potential, disturbing connections of ordinary life.

Your eyes can't see what is in front of you, but they can zoom in to see the impossible, the liquid in the gynecological syringe.[2] The passive tense haunts her telling; the alien agent is invisible, and Christina, lullingly, becomes a patient, both grammatically and thematically: *I was touched, liquid was placed* . . . A disorienting split opens between an index and the object it should point to; you smell smoke but there is no fire. There is a fog but it issues from nowhere. You feel the fog inside your mind, and you see it filling the room . . . and there is only the memory that comes back to possess you, or the memory of your body itself, the burning of your ovaries. They stole her hybrid daughter.

"It's like when human scientists tag those animals to study them," Mary says, "The animals don't know what's going on either." The human being is linked to lab animals, and the invaded, torn-up earth, and the medicalized sexuality of bodies (see also Brown 2007). This is a dominant theme of the standard abduction memory.

But this was not the only kind of story to tell here. The experiencers group was also a space to tell all kinds of stories that no one could pin down. Yes, some memories contained fragments of the standard abduction narrative; they were part of that field of uncanny public memory, wherever in the world of signs it came from. But in the Hillview Experiencers Group, many stories were wild, shifting, shapeless, half-recalled illustrations of something everyone here recognized and just called *weird*.

Like the clinical abduction narrative in Budd Hopkins's books, here too people told about a sense of violation, being watched, tracked, and invaded. That was not the only feeling, though. There was also an exhilarating, terrifying, amazing *other real* out there. People just said: *There is more going on*. The *more* was shorthand for many things. It included open narrative form, political distrust, and hinted-at sorrows and injuries that could never be told with beginnings and ends. The *something more* was a way that people sometimes briefly spoke of being misunderstood growing up, chafing at rules. It was being told to shut up and contain yourself in childhood, when no one understood that you saw things differently, that you had questions, longings, and a hinting sense that *this here* could not be everything. It was being told your terrors were silly and your desire to read books was a waste of time. And on top of that, *more* was an intimation of some kind of nascent shift that was happening even as we spoke. Things were changing, but it was a change that couldn't be articulated all the way.

Sometimes people resist the standard abduction story. One day, an older woman comes to tell her story. *Something* had happened to her in childhood, she says. She's half-remembered it all her life, putting it aside because there was no place in her world to think it. And she had never known what to make of it. Now she sits in the circle surrounded by supporters, with her hands folded, and she says:

> *I think what they were doing was, I think they put something through my navel.*

A man in the group nods expertly. He knows the standard abduction narrative and he raises his eyebrows from across the circle, saying, *Mmmm hmmm.* The woman continues her story of what she calls the Beings, ignoring his interjection, and he interrupts her again to explain what was happening in her case:

Man: Well what they were *doing* was reproducing our kind—
Woman:—No, I don't feel that's what they did to me.
Man: They were reaching down to your ovaries—
Woman: No, they went through my navel.
Man: Right. That's the tricky way of getting eggs.

If you aligned yourself with Hopkins's account as the monologic version of alien violation, the man's explanation made sense. But the rest of the group did not accept his explanation; no one confirmed him, or gave other cues of support. Instead everyone returned attention to other idiosyncratic details of the woman's specific experience. They believed she had an experience with *something* alien, but they believed even more that she was the one to define her own experience. People here often discussed the clinical abduction narrative at other times, from the story of Betty and Barney Hill onward. And people were always willing to listen to any ideas about what aliens might be up to;

reproducing the human species was always considered a possibility. But at this moment no one agreed with this man's authoritative explanation. For here, his small, fleeting performance was itself a medicalizing stance. He was trying to finalize the woman's open-ended and gauzy tale. For the group, this man's confident comment was shot through with gendered authority. He was on the wrong side. The experiencers group implied that clinical alien abductions resonated with unmarked moments of medicalized hegemony in everyday life.

## Looking for UFOs: Science Talk, Experience Talk

Some UFO researchers seek empirical evidence of UFOs and aliens, and sometimes they find it: dried rings of grass where the UFO set down and burned the earth, and the animals won't go near it. Peculiar scraps of metal; the body and its mysterious scars—things that never seem finally conclusive, but still raise a doubt. Some UFO researchers are determined to find the hard truth about UFOs. They follow a trail of bread crumbs, determined to identify the flying object at last.

But empirical finality is not what drives the support group. Here the ground you explore is part of your own experience that you can't tell anyone else—the middle-of-the-night memories, the synchronicities, the strange small face that you could never shake, the feeling that might just have been a dream. Or sometimes you retell stories you've heard, giving them extra weight when they're told in the context of the group, letting weird things begin to add up. Betsy says, "I talked to a friend the other day—he told me about this one thing that happened when I was a kid and I just went WHEEEP! He remembered being awakened as a kid by a bright white light coming out of his sister's room. She was asleep, or so he thought. And *for some reason*, even though this bright light was in her room, he *just went back to bed.* And then he woke up and the bright light was in *his* room. Isn't that *weird?*

Everyone understands what is meant by *the weird stuff*. It embraces a whole field of meaning. From inside *the weird*, a UFO is always immanently unidentified. It is a manifestation of the unfinalized and the liminal. That is the point. You can feel, as Kapchan has put it, that "the imagination is active and agentive" (2007: 28). We become suffused with a sense of the potential in the real.

What feels *weird* is the light that came in your window as a child and held you rapt in its glow; a sound, a glimpse, a feeling that something was real but at the same might just have been a dream. It is a disorienting doubt about your own bearings. It is when you find a playing card on the street and the same card turns up again later on the bus. *The Queen of Spades, what does it mean? . . . Must be the UFOs.* It is when you wake up in the middle of the night for no reason, and find your jewelry inexplicably removed and laid out on the pillow beside you. What happened? *Maybe it was UFOs.* An acquaintance with a flat affect who seems to *know things* without explanation, a snail on the porch that left no slimy residue as a trace as it crept away like a normal snail should do . . .

And it was, in retrospect, your strange reaction to something that wasn't quite right. It was being afraid of a seemingly small thing, or being too calm in the face of the incongruous, just going back to bed despite that light in your sister's room. Often what made something really *weird* was the very fact of not talking about it, until now—as if the event created its own silence that could break into the social only in the context of supporters.

> POLLY: One night I was in the car with my brother and his friends. We got about between "Grayville" and "Colton"[3] and it was dark and there was this really bright white light. Brighter than a star or a planet, it was like this big around, it went *whoop*. And then it was *gone*. And we never talked about it again.
>
> ME: Why not? Everyone says how they never talked about it again.
>
> POLLY (in a hushed, awed voice): *I don't know.* Isn't that *weird* though? *We never talked about it again.*

All these things registered as signs of *the weird*. And when people talked about a weird thing, they said it *seems like UFOs*. Here, a UFO was not a simple flying object from an as yet unidentified source in outer space. Instead it was an unfinalizable index to the open-ended weird.

We tell these things you don't say anywhere else. Madeline says that aliens come into her room, every night, she can't sleep; her husband won't listen to her. But the other night he screamed, "Don't take her, leave her alone!" and she awoke paralyzed to see a monstrous black shape above her, her husband swinging wildly at it. Next thing she knew it was morning, but *he won't discuss this nonsense.* She says she is scared, scared. She smokes pensively, incessantly, her candy-colored yellow hair falling over her long pale face and her blue eye shadow. Bob used to see UFOs when he was a little boy and the family lived overseas—they moved around, military family. And now, he says, his own three-year-old son is getting visits too.

And Berta, who emigrated from Austria, has seen lots of UFOs. Now she's blind, can see only the vaguest suggestion of light, but there's one thing and one thing only she can see as clear as day, not like an image but really see: it's an alien who looks like a beautiful man with black hair, and who uncannily appears at bus stops, malls, whenever she needs help and drives her home. Other people see him too so he's real, but, she says, *he is not human.*

There are a few blind people in the overlapping UFO communities, all of whom used to be able to see. Mary is always there with her dog. We often go to her house, the spare house of a person who has been blind for a long time. She remembers things she used to see, long ago, things she used to love: a rock she held in her hands, and it was so pretty, it felt like something magic. She doesn't talk much about herself but one day she abruptly says:

> I have been taken to a planet with three moons, I have been taken to Israel, I have been taken to Paris.

People here say: *This is not the stuff that science can explain.* They say: *Yeah, you could go over to MUFON,* the UFO research group where members dream after scientific evidence. In Hillview, there is in fact considerable overlap between MUFON and the Experiencers Support Group. There are shared members, and an ongoing, active social and discursive connection; indeed, the experiencer's group originally grew out of MUFON. But still. The support group folks say that MUFON members talk *nuts and bolts* of UFOlogy very well; they want to discuss measurements, rates of speed, bits of mysterious metals that analysis proves came from outer space. But, the Experiencers say with a smile: hey, if you want to tell the MUFON folks about your *weird stuff*—the stuff you can never prove—*well, proceed at your own risk.*


## Nuts and Bolts

Speech genres are not fixed or inert containers waiting to be filled by talk (cf. Bakhtin 1981, 1986); nonetheless, ways of speaking mark your stance. Nelson, a passionate MUFON member who never attends the Experiencers group, sits next to me at his friend's kitchen table one afternoon. We are here, planning MUFON-related events, and we are all stuffing dozens of flyers into envelopes to publicize an upcoming national UFO convention that's going to be held in Hillview. A well-known expert who writes about government conspiratorial covering-up of UFOs is going to be the keynote speaker; he has a degree in physics. His science credential, as well as his widely circulating book outing a major UFO cover-up, makes him a respected celebrity in UFOlogical worlds. And for some MUFON members a kind of heightened scientistic style comes into many registers of verbal talk. (By scientistic, I mean mimetic of scientific discourse, or in the "style of" science.) Here, in the friend's kitchen preparing materials for the conference, Nelson and I continue our ongoing talk.

> Me: What you saw, you feel like it *was* a UFO then?
> Nelson: But even if it was at 500 feet, I'd still have to classify
> it as nocturnal lights, because I could see *nothing* more
> than light *at any time*.
> Me: Just—
> Nelson: Let's put it this way. By my standards, it falls under
> the classification of UFO, because I saw something very
> strange, over a TWENTY-FIVE MINUTE PERIOD, I saw, what
> my brain translated to me, as FOUR (pause) DIFFERENT
> (pause) vehicles, if you will, if that's a good term to use,
> four of the three different types, four vehicles of three dif-
> ferent types, (pause) *doing strange things*.
> Nelson's friends laugh a little: *Lord it takes him so long to tell
> his story*. They rib him a bit. *Go on . . .* they say, fondly.
> Nelson: (His voice grows breathy.) I mean, stuff that I've never
> SEEN before . . . never in my LIFE have I seen a light do
> THIS number! (He gestures abruptly, making a quick right
> angle motion with his index finger.) Just shoot out, just out
> from apparently another light, and then just stop. And that
> happened twice . . . Okay, there was a dull (pause)
> fluorescent-looking light up there. It wasn't a bright light.
> It didn't fit. I wouldn't admit to it not being anything that
> would normally be explainable . . . until these lights shot
> out of it.

For Nelson, this strange light is "a UFO," something from another world, something amazing whose capacities exceed the constraining physics of our world. It is a light but it is dull, something hard to imagine with our own technology. There is no doubt, here, that the object exists not only outside our ordinary technological capacities, but also independent of his own consciousness. It is for now unidentified, but perhaps one day, if we are prudent and thorough, we *might* identify such things with science. This flying object need not be unidentified forever.

Nelson's speech style performs his epistemological stance. It shows he is cautious with facts, does not jump to conclusions; he shows he is a man who presents empirical data, not imaginary speculation. He talks with metascientistic care to document even his own observation process: *what my brain translated to me.* He calls the strange light a UFO because it is necessary to label it as unidentified, given its transgression of our known physics, the fact that "it didn't fit," but he is so careful about it: "*I wouldn't admit to it not being anything that would normally be explainable.*" His words form a complicated pile of doublings and difficult foldings. And then his own wonder infuses his scientistic talk, leaves him speechlessly searching in the piles of words. His reach for science is fueled by awe.

Nelson sees that the UFO moves outside the laws of our physics, but the basic rules of objectivity remain intact for him. The UFO here does not violate the existence of rules, but proves only that the object itself must come from a somewhere else. It is like Todorov's (1977) sense of the "marvelous" strange things that make sense according to the rules of their own marvelous world.

But in the Experiencers group it is different. People say, *You don't have to prove anything here.* Out there, in the bigger world, people mock you for speaking the truth of what you know; they deny you. People call you nuts, they always have. Outsiders try to pin down your open-ended self. They call you crazy, they say you're on drugs—*they go what have you been drinkin' or smokin'.* Yeah, says Hanna, like I was smoking or drinking when I was six years old—that's when the creatures started coming to surround her sleeping body. Well, says Emmalyn, no one calls you crazy here. *The weird stuff is real—yeah, whatever the hell that means!*

The real here itself is a shifting sign, constantly produced and dismantled; it can never be pinned down or summed up. *Out there,* they try to deny you. *In here*, the main thing is that for once you are going to be believed and heard while you swim head-on into the weird.

## The Flight of the Ordinary

Here is something we know in the support group: Something can take you outside your body, so you are floating above it and looking down. It can take apart your sense of the real and abduct your sense of an integrated point of view.

> I was um looking down on my body and I still had long hair.
> And at nine years old I had short hair with bangs
> and my hair had turned dark.
> So I was probl'y six seven eight years old.
> And I remember another dimension looking down on me, my
>     body;
> and here's this aggravating irritating look on my—
> on this little girl's face, which is me.
> . . . and as a child I thought I was in a field.
> But I could not have been in a field because there were no—
> was no grass, and there were no trees, so I don't know where I
>     was,
> but I'm looking down on this body.

Sandy remembers this from forty years ago. "Another dimension" is looking down "on this little girl . . . which is me." She says the look on her childhood face is not "aggravated," it is "aggravating," as if she is finding it "aggravating" now to see this child from above. Is she now aggravated along with her former self? Or are her verb tenses just slipping along with her disoriented point of view? Here, her use of the third person recalls the "projective 'I' of trance" that Urban describes (1986); the first-person pronoun indicates another character, not the embodied "speaker" but the character he's become through trance. That kind of disorientation is also a sign that it might be UFOs.

Joanne came to the group and told us this memory. She introduced her story:

This is the most realistic memory I have. The only thing I can say for SURE that happened. I'm just SURE that it happened.

I'd already gone to bed that night
And the first thing I was aware of,
I was just coming to consciousness,
Just like when you wake up.
And I was kind of playing,
And it was kind of like being weightless.
Kind of like one of those astronauts,
in one of those antigravity rooms.
Only I was in my living room . . .
And then I came to full awakeness.
And the first thing I asked myself was,
Am I in my material body?
And immediately the answer came to me:
Yes, you are.
And the next thing I knew
There was like this pull,
Like a suction above my head,
And I immediately started floating up
Straight through the ceiling.
And the next thing I know,
I'm still floating up
And I'm looking up
And seeing Hillview below me.
I don't know exactly what time it was
But it was just about to dawn,
And it was still really gray
And the sun hadn't peeked over yet,
But just enough so that you could see pretty clearly,
It was just about darker than twilight.
And I could see trees and houses and buildings and everything.
When I looked to the sides there was a panoramic view.
Everywhere I looked
There were other people floating up,
Hundreds if not thousands of people.

I remember there was this one man and he was the one closest
    to me,
And he had on this really fine business suit
—the kind you think would cost maybe a thousand dollars

—business double-breasted suit, and he had on a hat and he
  was carrying a briefcase.
And I remember the back of his suit flapping in the breeze.
I was really enjoying the ride, just like a kid,
I thought, this is fun!
Until I looked up,
And when I looked up I saw this circular craft that looked gray
  on the outer edge
But underneath there was this entire circular area
that was entirely filled in with this yellow molten lava
Looking, it looked like a living light, or a living lava, I had a
  sense that it was hot.

I looked up at it and I thought *That must be where I'm going.*
I said to myself *Don't get scared.*
But then I said to myself *I can't help it—I'm really scared.*

Joanne's memory starts out performing the liminality of the experience; it is neither dream nor waking, everything is gray. Many alien
abduction stories begin in the time between sleep and waking, but in
Joanne's story, we don't hear the standard abduction memory of clinical little gray aliens. The group is not judging Joanne's story based on
its corroboration of other, already entextualized standard abduction
memories. Instead of corroboration, there is a resonant truth that
makes affective sense: a vision of escaping the ordinary. The "businessmen," in expensive suits, are all along for this "ride" into a *something
else.* As it rises, everything begins to pleasurably dislocate into a placid
Magritte-like surrealism.

The ordinary realm that she said she "played with" leaving behind
her still saturates the story. She is never in a really different imagistic
realm; the uncanny is always familiar, shot through with what you
know. The businessmen are floating up in the air with her, as still as

inanimate images, with details like a "fine" suit tail flapping in the breeze. The emotion in the memory comes from that transition—the joy of escape without consequence ("this is fun!"—"like a ride!") and then collapses into refusal. The UFO is strange, but evokes images of familiar dread with its hot, living lava. Hell? Technologies of—what? No, she does not want to go there.

What happened next we never know. The next person told a weird memory. But the group accepted Joanne's story with an acknowledgment—*Yes that is weird*—and an acceptance that the real is made up of many iterations of containment and a wish for flight.

Opening this genred space to speak about *the weird* sparks a capacity to remember things. Memories fit the open shape you are given here. As I sit on my metal folding chair, ambiguous images fill my mind and I begin to *remember things* from childhood. It was not that I had ever forgotten them, I felt, but here they were, gleaming in my mind's eye. A vague sense of a disturbance would shape itself into potential story form. Now I told the image that came to mind. *I think I was a young child, standing on a balcony of a hotel. was I in Florida? I think it was Florida? And I saw a giant circular thing flying close to the balcony, shaped like a wheel with lights all along the sides . . . and I think at the time it is a ride of some kind but it's flying.* I stop there. Did this really happen? Did I dream it? Was the image conjured by the talk in which I now steeped myself? The image does not fit into any larger narrative of my life; it is an isolated image trying to become a story. Did I transpose parts of it from movies, or from the talk in this group, or layer memories of a childhood carnival ride onto a movie image of a UFO? Did I see a UFO? Everyone listens, nods, takes it in. I want to be honest; I say: *I doubt this really happened.* Yes, they nod. Fine. Doubt, too, fits in this room.

Later I call my sister and try to tell her about this weird thing. *Did that happen?* I ask her. She would have shared the balcony in Florida; what does she think? She laughs, *Oh, one of those kinds of childhood memories, who the hell knows.* I agree and shift back to my ordinary comfortable stance toward the real. We talk about other things then, the stuff of life we're grounded in. It's not so odd for anyone to have a flash of the weird, but in the experiencers group the flash becomes an identity, a cultivated speech genre, an epistemology, a politics, and a kind of sacred ground.

# The Earth

In these stories, the earth is poeticized as the ground of the ordinary—a "natural" ground that, in the disorienting realm of the modern unnatural, is said to be plundered and lost.

How do contemporary myths imagine the natural world, and poeticize the earth? In the rationalized landscapes of America, nature is not necessarily poeticized through storied sites of specific emplacements, embodiments, or memories. Instead, nature is spoken of as a site of nostalgia, a lost home, where embodiment and memory are achingly present only in their absence. People often move to and away from Hillview; storied nature, families, and "roots" are elsewhere. Or, perhaps, they're nowhere. What is left is a longing for a more "real" place, a more "natural" home, and an earth that was once uncolonized.[4]

On summer nights, a few of us would sleep out in the undeveloped land that stretched behind Nicholas and Dale's place, where we'd lie side by side to talk the night away and search the skies for UFOs. Around our clearing was what Nicholas and Dale called "the woods," nature on the working-class edge of the city. We knew there were hunters in there, probably shooting at raccoons and squirrels; and we could hear the gunshots, though it wasn't much of a woods. But we'd tramp through unbroken briars, Dale leading the way with his walking stick, huffing and puffing, until the path became a deer path; and we would get tangled and lost until we found the clearing to lie in. Then we talked in the faint surrounding thrum of a distant highway, with everything cast in the nocturnal glow not of the moon but of the government-sponsored microchip consortium across the woods. Some of the UFO friends worked there.

It's all happening too fast, Janet says. The earth is overwhelmed. The animals are disappearing, things are going down. Just look at the news.

Nothing is what it used to be.

Sometimes the aliens are storied as benevolent guardians warning us of our own technology spinning out of control, and other times they are sinister high-tech thieves of human nature. But always, these are stories of a too-present realm of the unnatural, urgently erupting into the antinatural zones of postmodernity to point—nostalgically—to the eclipse of nature. The sense of crisis is palpable; the earth is felt to be veering on its own axis, overcome by pollution and the weight of nuclear bombs awaiting the day of flight. Then the *earth itself* is often storied as a subject, a feeling body violated both by aliens and high-tech humans. Look at all the signs: earthquakes, fires, storms, and floods. Gaia's gearing up for the big one. The earth is mouthing off.

Polly says one day: *I try and put it in the big picture. A lot of people feel they've lost control. It's all overmechanized, this too-technical society where the least little thing you want to do is beyond your control.*

## God Comes on a Spaceship

At the same time, for some of us here, the old sacred stories are fading, falling under the authority of science. When Nicholas was a boy his people could be possessed by demons. That was long ago, when he lived with what he called his "Bible thumper" family. He left a place that constrained him with its certainty. Aliens take over your body, but Nicholas recalled talk of possessions from another symbolic world that also meant struggle for control over the body (Csordas 1990). When he talked at home about his alien encounters, his grandmother thought he'd met Satan, and she tried to make him drop to his knees and pray. Then he would perform a different encounter for us, one between the grandmother's Christian voice and his own: "Get on your knees boy," he said in his grandmother's voice; in his own: "I don't care, I'm not gonna do it!" he said, dramatically alternating voices between grandmother and himself.

Sometimes Nicholas said he was going to shake it all off, he said; he had changed, he knew there were UFOs and aliens and weird stuff, and no one from home understood it. Sometimes he seemed to say he'd moved on. But other times he tried to make a bridge back and connect what he knew now to what they know back home.

> NICHOLAS SAID: Because the Bible is written in a way . . . for people of that day, of that time, to understand. And then for science to translate into later periods of time, for where *we* can understand. Why God appeared upon a cloud, to me, somebody appears to anybody on a *cloud*, they're just not floating on air, they're on *something*.
>
> SUSAN: Mmm.
>
> NICHOLAS: God comes on a spaceship.

I mean, a cloud, appears to uh—when Jesus came back—on a cloud— and appeared to Mother Mary—or no, Mary Magdalene. At the well. She didn't believe it was Jesus. And then he also went to Doubting Thomas. Doubting Thomas didn't believe it was him.

He told him to feel his wounds and his palms, or actually there's no muscle here [pointing to his own palms, then to his wrists]. When they nailed people it was right in the wrist, which is right next to the palm, cause you have that bone right there that kept it from slipping off on the spikes [holding his wrist up]. You get nailed in the palm, the muscles'd tear and fall off, so they nail it in the wrist. That has been proven; the Shroud of Turin showed that.

His story foregrounds the crucified body, the physical intensity in the violence of the cross. He still is immersed in the crucifixion, though it's now an ambivalent immersion. And at times—*no, Mary Magdalene*—he is beginning to forget it all.

*       *       *

Yes, anarchy is coming, and Carla can feel it in her bones. The day is coming when we won't need people to tell us what to do; soon we won't take it. The insiders in Washington won't release the information about UFOs. Carla says, *This is a police state here.* She says one day: I want to move away from America; I'll move to Canada. There in Canada the people are real, not phony like the ones down here, not so greedy and mean. . . *I'm just getting that the people care about the real stuff, up there.* One day, as I'm walking into her house, I hear Carla, Brian and Mary talking: the government's hiding information on UFOs and trying to keep us all in line, but boy, are we mad. *Fucking mad!* she yells as I walk in. *You can say fuck here!* She laughs a powerful laugh and then sings: *rev-o-lution!!!*

Here, stories of felt marginality are constantly resocialized, piled up with other stories in an unflinching tolerance for others in the group. Carinna had no UFO stories, and never talked about uncanny experiences, but she came to the group through Nicholas. *Something is wrong,* I wrote in my notes after I first met her; she told jokes that didn't quite work, interrupted stories with nonsequiturs, and the group never picked up to build on what she said. But she felt comfortable here; and everyone was comfortable with her around. Then one night, out in the field watching for UFOs, she suddenly asked, "Has anyone else had a serious head injury?" It seemed like a fraught moment, but everyone simply began telling their minor head injury stories without missing a beat. There were stories of concussions and black eyes. Carinna finally filled in the details:

> I was on my bike, no helmet.
> Afterwards I told my dad, I knew I wasn't going to die.
> My dad said: You mean you hoped.
> I said, no, not hoped, knew.
> I saw the pickup coming straight at me
> and I thought, *here comes a change . . .*

Then someone chimed right in to join her about head injuries. "My mother said I fell off the bed but I wouldn't be surprised if she hit me," and someone else said his brother whacked him good with a belt buckle. And then Janie said she was in a car accident once too, and her friend died; Janie had to spend months in rehab learning how to walk again. I wonder why it happened to me? she said mildly. These were the very same words she'd said so many times before, in a much more dramatic, intensely searching way, about the tiny, weird things that seemed to occur around her and that made life uncanny: Why was a bird's egg directly in her path? Why did acorns form a perfect circle on her step? Why did it happen to me!—as if she were at the center of a vast design, with signs made of tiny bits out of order. Now Janie just shrugged, her voice taking on the register of everyday acceptance. No one made Carinna's story of brain injury seem extreme, strange, or even more significant than anyone else's. Storytellers closed ranks around her, brought her into a circle of narratives made similar by their place inside a felt outside. This space for the *unheimlich* was, in fact, a home.

## CHAPTER 6

# It All Comes Together

## *Power, Containment, the Dream of Escape*

Long ago, "Randall"[1] was a little boy in Kentucky. Then his father and mother moved the family from the hard land where the farm wouldn't take, from the place where they were poor, and still used a plow with a horse. They moved to find work in the cold factories of Detroit—a move made by many poor southerners and one Randall, who was ten at the time, says he never got over. It was a move that left him feeling permanently adrift, until he came west and started his life over *like a pioneer*. Before he found the sunshine of Nevada, though, he was caught in the scar left by the wound of his family's uprooting. He said:

> When I was ten my parents moved from Kentucky to Michigan.
> And whatever roots I had at that age it was in Kentucky.
> You know, young people usually stay around where their mother and dad are.
> I guess, I guess that's the law.
> Susan: Oh yeah, you were only ten.
> Randall: But I went in the service in 1957. When I got out of the service
> I told Mom and Dad, I said,
>
> I'm a-goin down to Kentucky, I'm gonna head down there.
>
> But when I got down there as a young adult

I didn't like Kentucky any more than I did Michigan.

I went back to Michigan cause there's no work in Kentucky.
I went back to Michigan
and got in the carpenter trade. Went back to Michigan.
And I hated it for thirty years.

In 1979 I left.

Then I—I wasn't happy, I wasn't satisfied, I didn't feel like I
    was at home.
I just didn't like where I was living. No matter where—

Before we were married I went up just south of Chicago, Indi-
    ana,
I got a job at U.S. Steel up there at first,
Then I went to work at American Steel.
I was running machines, you know,
drill press, you know,

just various production machines. And . . .
I didn't like it there any better'n I did Michigan.
So I went back.

My oldest daughter was born in Hammond Indiana.
We went back to Michigan in '61, I believe.
I went to work at General Motors Truck and Coach.
I was a press operator. Ran machines.
Any dummy can run machines.
You put the stop in there,
You push the button!

Then I was ending my second marriage.
And I had already decided, my God,
I was in Michigan,

And God I hated that place.
There was MOSQUITOES
And BLACK FLIES
And DEER FLIES

And TICKS.
I hated that.

I hated that.

I went back to Michigan.

I started an addition on my house,

Still had to do some things, put the toilet in.

Well it was *her* house [the wife he was leaving].
It's not right that I should leave a job undone.
It was my job, my idea.

I took two months to finish the job.

Then I packed all my stuff and said: *Adios.*
And I headed west.
And I've never, never been sorry one day.

I wouldn't *live* in that country back there.
Not a day!
My dad retired in '85;

they moved back to Kentucky.

As you know we were down there recently for my sister's wed-
    ding anniversary.
And you look at that place.
My god it's depressing.
You got trees all around!
And it's *wet*!
And you walk out in the morning, and your *feet's wet*!
All the dew!

The humidity!
Everything is rotting.
Ever since the beginning of time!

More than any other kind of personal story, people stopping to talk, to have a beer or a coffee and rest a while in these wide desert places, told about their travels. They told long, long narratives that could sound sometimes like an itinerary of surfaces. *I went here, and here and here, and here I had a flat tire, and then I went here and here . . .*

Or: where are you from? *We lived here, we were in the service so we moved here and then we moved here and then here . . .*

Or *We lived in a house with four bedrooms and a Jacuzzi, then we lost it, we moved in with my parents and we couldn't take that so then we hit the road, we lived in this town, but that didn't work out, and then here . . .*

Ambivalent meanings spin out in tales of mobility and *staying put,* of freedom and home. For years of his life, Kentucky became an imaginary home Randall would someday reclaim in the long, lived-out odyssey and the idea of a return *one day . . .* this was the story he dreamed to himself through the cold years up north. But when he got back there to Kentucky it just wasn't right. The place that stayed behind was overloaded and too dense, permanently decaying but never burned clean by its own consumption. *Rotting from the beginning of time.* There was never a fresh beginning; it was already too much before it began. This place was a deep well of too much rootedness, but a rootedness he was no longer part of. It was the opposite of the clear empty dry new possibility of the West, a place where nothing was used up yet, nothing could become rotten here, nothing was even yet ripe.

Because he had traveled too far, there was no hometown left for him to dream about. And that was both a rupture and a liberation. As everything unraveled he built a house in Michigan that he would never live in; and when it was done, and he was in a wide open space with nothing left, he headed west, which is of course a story whose outlines were already in place, the grooves already laid down . . .

Now he felt free. He said once in Nevada it took him only three days to "acclimatize" to the heat. He drove around, ecstatically free; and on the second day he found work. He learned how to adjust to the burning sun of Las Vegas. There were tricks you learned to really live and work here. *You lay your saw in the shade* so its metal won't burn you when you pick it back up again. You do the same with all your tools, why you just *lay 'em in the shade.* And from that strange moment when he jumped wholeheartedly into his own rootlessness, he began to settle down. Picked up tools to live in a new way and would not get burned.

Pat and Joe, the married owners of the Inn, had moved here from elsewhere too, had stories and roads behind them, and they had settled deeply in. Pat had travel stories of her own, and she had also come to start over here, in Nevada, after years of settling down and then plucky starting over, making new worlds: crossing the country on buses, or cars that coast the last miles home on fumes. Waitressing, working as a short-order cook, counting on fate and luck to see her over the gaps inevitably left by any life put together with hard work. Luck followed Pat, just at the right time, when all the hard work seemed to collect an extra little something from the universe to get her through a tight spot. Like the extra pennies she'd forgotten in her closed bank account; or the time a total stranger came up to her in an all-night diner and just gave her a hundred dollars, and said, *Get those kids home safe*. Now, married all these years, Pat and Joe were generators of income for many people, civically involved with life in the county, and pillars of the community.

The Little A'Le'Inn was making them successful. Now they weren't just scraping by. They were buying a bit of land in Rachel. They had added on a lot to the café, and bought a bigger trailer to live in next door. Pat said she couldn't afford to give her daughter a real girly room before. Mary was grown now, lived a few trailers down, and worked with her mom in the café. Now that second bedroom was filled with a stiff, ruffled bedspread and curtains, for when their granddaughter stayed with them for long periods. But the new trailer still was rough, had a few holes waiting for fixing some time when they weren't working all day and night in the café. When people asked Joe why he didn't get a house instead, he countered that this was what he *liked* better—what do you need *that* for? A house was a sign of not moving. In Nevada, people told me, there are so many trailers you have to pay home property tax if yours has a permanent foundation. It's affordable; but also, good to know you can always just haul it and move away whenever you want.

Margie fondly says Randall is a preacher behind the bar. His father really was a preacher, back in Kentucky. One afternoon I sit beside Randall on a barstool in the near-empty café while he drinks his Old Milwaukee and strokes his bushy gray beard. He's already done his work for this morning, using his carpenter tools in the shed out back to make items to sell in the gift shop: he's wired a lamp with an alien head base, poured the little plaster spacemen into molds before gluing them to magnets. Now he's preaching *the way things are* in the cadences of revelation, as he says:

The powers that be
are every day striving
to destroy the Constitution . . . And they will.
And they *have* done it.

When I see 'em coming up that road I'm ready. I'll go out there
    and meet 'em on that road.
I keep this gun right here on the bar. I'll meet 'em in their
    tanks.
They're coming to take our guns, to make us their slaves.
They've already *built* the concentration camps.
Well, I'd rather die on my feet than live on my knees.
They are into the occult.

On the back side of the one-dollar bill on the left-hand side—
    see here, there's a circle and a pyramid,
the pyramid of Giza,

the all-seeing eye of Lucifer or Satan
or whoever you would like to put in that position. When this
    *pyramid* is in place,
then the New World Order or Satan
will be in charge.

You know symbolism is everywhere in our daily lives.
From what I've learned
and what I understand

this evil is set about to take over the world. I have to believe,
I have to pray to God,

that they won't succeed this time.

Cause the tyrannical people that are in charge, well, if they in
    fact do usher in
this New World Order,

the people have never known slavery
such as they will suffer

under the hands of these people.
That's my firm belief.
The people of this country have no idea, in my opinion,
  what's coming.


How can I understand this talk, in light of Randall's sanity, his decency and kindness?

Why is the fabulous prophecy of a white man from Kentucky a montage of these specific tropes, in which the Satan of boyhood sermons is infused with still-restless images of slavery and concentration camps, co-articulating signs of some unnamed power watching *the little man* through the all-seeing eye of the dollar?

Here again he makes connections both by spinning outward into the similar images, and also by spinning inward, to the occult nestings of meaning inside words. There are secret etymologies that show you more connections. As Randall puts it:

Well they worship the *owl*,
because the owl can see in the *dark*,
so therefore he's very wise . . .


You know when you talk about college graduates, they become
    *alum*ni;
*illuminated.*


This all ties together, and it's, it's
it's amazing . . .


You might see the uncanny in Randall's feeling for what Taussig (1997) calls the magic of the state, and in the amorphous social discontent that refuses class consciousness. You might see it in his identification with master tropes of freedom and individuality and ownership and nationalism from well inside an intersubjective sense of being generally *out of place*, just *screwed over*. When a man first came into the bar testifying the New World Order and the devious plot of all the powers that be, Randall says it stopped him dead in his tracks. It was his conversion narrative. It hit him like a bolt of lightning, he said. Because like he said, all his life he just *knew* that *something wasn't right*. This man gave him the words. The neighbors too, ranchers or farmers with stable habits and straight ways, or perhaps hay throwers, machinists, miners, well-diggers or just dreaming drinkers and settled down drifters—all curse that far-off federal power when they think of how *they* can come and just seize a man's land, land that was bought and paid for with a man's own money. Or a woman's—that one lady holed up in her place and would not *budge*, and the ATM could not get her out of there for weeks. But finally the government just storms in and seizes your house and property because they say they need if for "something else." And right here in the shadow of the military—now, you don't blame them *up there* in uniform, doing their job.

Sometimes when Randall preaches, the congregation in the bar chimes in with its amens. Here Randall was talking about picking up a Mexican hitchhiker who was here because he couldn't get work at home. NAFTA wasn't helping the poor Mexicans and now they had to come up here and get American jobs. But it wasn't the fault of the poor. You can't blame the Mexicans. He preaches and Lloyd responds from the pew of his barstool:

> Randall: It's not [the fault of] the people! It's not the people,
> it's the governments! It's our government,
> and their government—
> Lloyd: The governments!
> Randall: You got it!
> They are working hand in hand to enslave the people!
> We are all enslaved.

> Don't think for a minute that we are not.

> Jack: Oh I know we are. Oh I know that we are.
> Randall: And they are fast turning this country
> into a Third World country.
> Lloyd: Out for profit!
> Randall: A short time ago
> we were the number one country in the world.
> Lloyd (bitterly) We're number *twenty* now.
> Randall: We are the world's largest debtor nation! And this
>    didn't happen by accident!
> Lloyd: No, you know it didn't!

Lloyd chimes in with Randall, echoing him and building up the dialogic sermon, a chorus that echoed with the call-and-response traditions of churches, and that came directly out of the structure of Randall's talk itself, and the kind of space he made open up for the listener.

As for Lloyd, he was traveling the country. He says: *I came out of Vietnam a bleeder. And they won't accept any responsibility for it.* After he left the navy, he had worked as a school janitor, until one day he got a nosebleed and it would not stop. He was bleeding, and bleeding, and bleeding. In the hospital they had to they said to him: *Have you been exposed to any kind of chemical thing?* Then he remembered—spreading Agent Orange back in Vietnam.

Every few months he had to travel back to his home state, to try to get the disability he was entitled to legally. *They* were giving him a hard time. There had been a lawyer, there had been a senator trying to help. There had been talk of a group action. Class action suit. But none of it panned out. A disappointment if not exactly a surprise: *Nobody got a nickel out of them.*

He had been patriotic as a young man, but then his government had betrayed him. Just like, he said, *they wouldn't admit it to people who'd been screwed up by atomic exposure, until they all were dead.*

He talked without complaining about the details of his bleeding. It was unreal, he said. The bleeding poured from him when it began. He told about this time it happened, and that time in happened, in a calm, resigned voice that mapped out an itinerary of bleeding.

But his voice got animated afterward when he told me about the ghost who had appeared to him. There he was, over at the school where he was mopping up. He had closed every locker door, and *something* opened them up again. He had swept up a pile of papers and *something* took them out and lined them up, all in a row, neat as a pin. It made the hair stand up on his body. He *saw something* out of the corner of his eye . . . Something, *something* was there. He tells the story and I believe it; *something happened* beyond the struggle of ordinary life and he was able to witness it, and it was a shift it the real. Lloyd saw the traces of a ghost, and telling about it made his eyes light up.

It isn't that the ghosts aren't real (Gordon 2007). Sometimes, a sense of injustice develops into a structure of feeling—one suffused with desire, betrayal, injury, and a sense of vanishing potential. And then, sometimes the uncanny is itself the redemption—the *something more*, the part that escapes, the return of possibility beyond what you might have thought.

Sometimes what comes into view is the simultaneous terror of, and hunger for, just being taken away.


## An Abduction

Tina worked for a while in the Little A'Le'Inn's gift shop, a corner of the café lined with shelves of souvenirs. (Like most of the others here, her name and some details are altered.) Tina was in her fifties; thin as a rail, she always wore big dark glasses, an oversized T-shirt, and a visored cap marked with a UFO logo. While living in Andrewville, she said, she'd read about Rachel, Nevada, in a *Weekly World News* article—it said that aliens regularly came into the town to hang out at the Little A'Le'Inn. After seeing that article, Tina said she knew she had to move to Rachel. She made her way out here bit by bit, coming the last stretch on a three-speed bicycle. After she was here a while, she got a little camper to live in.

One day we are inside the town's Quonset hut—it is a fundraiser to buy a defibrillator for Rachel. It is a sweet event, a community gathering like many others in small towns where I have been. Someone has sewn a beautiful quilt to auction off for the benefit, and there is plentiful food. I have come over with two kids I'm watching, ages five and seven. The kids are dancing joyfully, running out to the swing set now and then, and there is a band; and Lloyd and Dan are laughing with Tina, playfully saying she is a hybrid, half-alien. And she agrees with them: *Yes, I am half alien.* She nods. I joke back: *Which half?* But then I realize she is dead serious. She answers: *Half alien on my dad's side.*

So then Tina and I go outside where we can talk.

The wind is blowing up dust and dry weeds, starting to fill our ears. She speaks a bit louder, so I can hear her over this wind. She says she's always known that she didn't belong here *on this particular planet. I was from somewhere else. And my parents weren't my real parents.*

We move around, getting out of the wind so I can hear her story. And she says she has *seen things*, at night, behind trees—the little grays with dark almond eyes. When she was a kid they were watching her and she was really afraid. She could tell no one. Grown-ups used to say: don't be silly, don't be afraid of the dark. But, she said, kids aren't being silly when they are really afraid, and they don't understand what it is.

The grown-up who said that is dead now, and anyway the people she was told were her parents were not really her parents. That is something she always somehow just knew, though when she was a kid she didn't understand why she had that knowledge. That is why they *treated her different*. And then she too had a conversion—not all at once, but little by little, when she realized why nothing ever felt right, she didn't fit, and little by little she started *going more and more to the UFO side*.

But now she knows, just knows, her real dad is here. And he knows that she is here, to find him. He is a gray alien, and they are keeping him at Area 51, holding him there. Every day, she says good morning and good night to him. Because she knows it, she feels it, and it is so, so strong.

*I have yet to see him*, Tina says, *but I think soon I will.*

The sunset now is turning the mountains orange and gold, makes them glow. Tina can hardly keep her eyes off them.

There's my famous Area 51 mountains, she says. *That's where my father is, and that's where I want to be.*

Her words come in a rush when I ask her if she thinks other people know about this. She says: people don't know what's coming. She says: it's not gonna be too cool when things go down with this New World Order thing. One of her friends has been has been telling her to get prepared, to get ready.

They are gonna come for people, find you wherever you're at. They have devices that can find you. There is no way you can hide from them, even underground. They will come and get you, and even now they are taking people, making them slaves, doing experiments on them, in the mountains of the West. And the people never come back.

I don't know what to say. I just murmur some dismay.

People disappear, she says again, and they never come back.

Even kids, teenagers. It's been happening for a long, long time.

I ask her about the missing kids. There was a pamphlet about them in the café.

—People sell the kids and teenagers as sex objects, she says. To other countries.

—Does that have anything to do with Area 51? I ask, confused. I still take her story for a causally organized narrative.

—No, I don't think so, she answers. It could. I don't think so.

In fact, her narrative is not organized causally. It is organized mimetically, a plot of contagious magic. She isn't talking about missing children because they are inside Area 51, although now that I mention it, it's possible . . . These things are linked because they are all affectively resonant images of captivity, chains of association making piled-up images of horror, in which the innocent are captured by unseen forces, never seen again. Again, the object of the story is the resemblance between the seemingly random and discrete captivities—the object is the rush of apophenia, the glimmer of a pattern in it all.

(The next day she gives me a gift from her camper: a tiny plastic box that has a recording inside, a high-pitched voice screaming "Let me out, Let me out of here." She laughs hard at it, the humor seizes her in deep kick of recognition. *Let me out! let me out of here!* cries the little recording; it gets to her, it's hilarious.)

*Who* is gonna come for people and take them away? I ask now.

She shakes her head. "The military, the government, the New World Order?" Her answer trails off in the tone of a question. It is not definable, or it would be something you could change. It is *they*, and no one knows exactly who they are.

Then Tina tells me about her three UFO experiences. The first one was in 1989, when she lived in a little town in another state.

And in the little town . . . lights went off one night. I knew
   then things from another world was out there.
I started talking to them,

communicating with them telepathically.

And somewhere in October or December or November of
   '89—october of '89—
there was an incident that happened.

My girlfriend's daughter came home from the lake.
She was working out there in the filling station.
Uncle Frank—her uncle Frank—brought her home.

And Alma, her mother, was over at my place. We were talkin'.
    And she come runnin' upstairs
and she says, Mom, Mom.

And I told Kristi, your mother's up here.
She come running in
and she says, Mom, Guess what.
Me and Uncle Frank saw a UFO.
And I says *really?*
And from what I understand, it was like a few seconds.
It went away—

just *wsssst*, out of sight.

And there was other witnesses that seen it,
but I really don't know if they reported anything. I don't know
    if they had it in the paper or what.

Then she tells me the story of her own abduction. Tina says,
—And then, towards November or December, *I* was taken up
    on a ship.
—You *were*? I ask.
—Yup. I wanted to go. I wanted to go with them and I didn't
    want to come back.
But evidently, I'm back. I'm still here.

For a second, I'm struck dumb by the word "evidently."

—What happened? I ask her.
Tina says—[and I've changed the names in her story, just as
    I've changed Tina's]—

It was late one night
Wee early hours of the morning.
I was asleep in bed.
I would hear this popping noise behind my left ear.
I would wake up but nothing was around.
And then there was a bluish white light . . .

and I got up and I went to my front room window, which was a
    picture window.
I looked up

and there was this great big huge ship,
bigger than a house.
Bigger than a football field.
It was round and silver.
And I had my robe on, and my pj's underneath.
And I went around my bookcase, and opened the door
and went downstairs.
I was barefoot.
And I went over the little rock yard

onto the sidewalk and out onto the street.
And I looked up.
When I looked up, I did like this:

[She raises her arms above her head]. And I wanted—
I says, *Take me.*
*I want to go.*
And as I went up I could feel it, as I was going up.
I was in awe; I really liked it.

And as far as what they *did* to me, I don't know.
That was blocked out.

All I remember is, I went up

underneath this great big huge round silver disc.

—Why didn't you want to come back? I ask her.

—Too much crap here on this planet, she says.
Too much cruelty to people.
People aren't kind to one another.
I mean, *these humans,*
they need to learn kindness,
to be kinder to people.
Not so violent,

not so much killing.

Well I've lived on this earth,
on this planet
for almost fifty-four years.
And I don't like it.
I feel I'm *caught in between,* in other words.
I've been here too long.
I'd rather not be here.

I'd rather be with my own kind . . .

My planet is gone. That's why I'm here on Earth.
It's totally destroyed.
—Is that gonna happen to Earth? I ask.

—Probably eventually.
The way things are doing, they're destroying everything . . .
there's not gonna be anything left for anybody.

I turn off my recorder and we begin to walk back in the heavy air left
by her story and her knowledge. And then she begins to talk more.

I can tell you something.

We don't have birth certificates like you humans do on earth.
We don't have money.
It is not cold
it is not hot
where I came from,
and yet I don't know exactly where.

My planet is gone. That's why I'm here on Earth.
Susan: Do you know what happened to your planet?
Tina: No. It's gone. Totally destroyed.

Tina and I were quiet; and the air was sad.
—There's my famous Area 51 mountains, she says, gazing at
    them as they go dark from orange.
—There they are, I say.

—That's where I'd rather be than anywhere else, she says.

Are you gonna stay living here in Rachel? I ask Tina a little
    later.
No, she says, I'm always on the move.
I never stay in one place too long at a time . . .
I don't know where I want to go or what I want to do.

She hugs the solid presence of her skinny frame in its huge T-shirt,
her lined face and the startling sorrow of her eyes obscured as usual by
dark glasses and the low bill of a UFO baseball cap.

But as she remembers and tells the story of her UFO abduction another self emerges, transformed by its desire for otherness, and by its
acceptance there. Suddenly she is not a lost middle-aged woman in a
baseball cap with the ruins of a life somewhere behind her. Her story
transforms her: she becomes a gothic figure: barefoot in a garden,
streaming with light, in a nightgown, her arms reaching up for the vehicle of sublime departure from *this place*. Earth.

Later I think of Randall's old Kentucky home *rotted from the beginning of time*. Sometimes Earth itself feels like that kind of home,
played out and too old . . . But from here in the desert sometimes there
is a sense of potential escape.

A few weeks later, Tina was leaving "this place"—Rachel—and
drifting again. But for a while, she'd settled here. She had made Rachel
her home. Someone passing through Rachel had sold her the little
camper to live in. The lights didn't work, and sometimes it didn't start
up, but inside she had everything she owned—knickknacks, a few
clothes, meaningful photos taped to the walls, and dozens of jars of
water drawn from the tap at the café, to survive on when things got
bad. She had parked the camper on the far side of Rachel, closer to the
Area 51 Research Center than to the café, and she would sit at night
with Lloyd and Danny. She had adopted a puppy from the Travis's litter
and kept it tied on a rope to the front of the camper to greet her when
she came home.

And then there was a conflict, and Tina said she would be moving
on again.

A few days later, she asked me to take her to get her driver's license,
though she'd been driving for decades without one, moving from place
to place.

And so I took Tina on out to Tonopah and sat with her in the gleaming, chilly office. It was quiet, empty except for a woman in pink holding a toy poodle in a matching dog sweater.

Tina hunched intensely over the driver's test, laboring on the questions of the law. I'd offered to help her study, but she said she'd read the manual and knew it all. But she did not pass; in the crunch, it was foreign material to her.

*We don't have birth certificates like you humans do on earth, we don't have money,* Tina had said about her own planet. For her, the driver's license was like those things: a charged sign, an ambivalent passport into the ordinary world and its random laws.

It made her quiet. On the long drive back to Rachel that day, we came upon the wild mustangs that run across federal land. They were grazing in the road and then running across the hills, their whole bodies alert to watch us. We pulled to the side of the road, got out and shut the doors softly behind us. There were no cars coming down the empty miles; we stood and watched the horses. Then Tina began to run after them.

I followed her. The mustangs were dangerous and Tina seemed not to care. She was getting close to the stallion and he wasn't running; he looked poised to kick. I took hold of her skinny arm, said we should stand back.

Back in the car she was a bit angry and silent. She was angry at me for stopping her from running away with those horses. She said she'd wanted to *just go.*

After a stretch of empty miles Tina announced a decision to leave Rachel. She was going to take her camper and move on out to Tonopah and park somewhere in the desert near the DMV and go back every day to the clean well-lighted office until she passed the test. Why not, she said, it's free. The test is free.

And soon after, she was gone.

I looked for her camper in the desert when I made other trips to Tonopah, but I never saw Tina again.


## The License

How are such fabulous stories shaped by the inarticulate disappointments of everyday life? And how do people make sense of power's twin effects: restriction and possibility, forces that co-articulate with un-canny simultaneity?

Uncanny stories are always haunted by questions. In the stories I am telling here, the most central question (and the most maddeningly elusive) hovers over the constant, porous interplay between seemingly binary oppositions: the real and the imaginary, and their more material correlates, containment and mobility, limitation and potential. How is the interplay of these oppositions lived, embodied, and saturated with social meaning?

Though I keep the above large questions in mind, and though they are haunted by the uncanny specter of UFOs, the stories I want to tell in the next section come back to think more about the mundane, ordi-nary figure of the license itself—an ordinary metaphor that performs the dialectical forces of restriction and possibility emanating from modern experiences of power.

It wasn't just Tina. In other talk too, it turned out that a topic of conversation that came up now and then was that several of the drifters who worked in the café had driven for years without driver's licenses.

The word *license* is polysemic like the word *range*, a word you hear all the time in the West, saturated with meaning. There is *open range*, the absence of fences, the emblem of freedom. There is Nellis Air Force Bombing and Gunnery Range, in which the range is supposed to desig-nate a place with definite boundaries, an area that does not leak out onto the life outside its span. The word contains the doubleness of the dialectical trope, containment and freedom.

The word "license" does too. It can suggest lawless freedom—a li-centious abandon. And there's also the sense of "license" as a degree of freedom that is ultimately shaped by its own containment. In this sense, freedom is meted out by the authority of the state in its markers: tags and documents, concrete indices to an abstract idea of a social contract with power. The physical license you hold in your wallet al-ways implies freedom to act, but maintains awareness of the law cir-cumscribing the action. It reminds the actor that freedom has been granted and that freedom can be taken away—by the magic of the state, or what others call the *powers that be*.

When it works, the agreement to move without anxiety inside a licensed realm seems natural for those whose imagined community includes the "we" of the representative-based state. Yet for those who don't feel part of the franchise, this ordinary zone of sanctioned free-dom feels strange. Bureaucratic signs and procedures grow fabulous, charged with overdetermined meaning; and the conflict between law and freedom, which is supposed to remain unmarked, can grow uncanny in its emergent visibility. The *source* of power is felt to be simultaneously hyperpresent and hidden. And its conflicts are expressed in a struggle for something like *poetic* license, which takes *the real* itself as the site of struggle.

Alongside the die-hard discourse against the licensing of guns, alongside the endless rumination about UFOs and what the government was hiding up there at Area 51, people talked, sometimes, about the anxieties raised by the Department of Motor Vehicles.

One afternoon, a café worker named Ken—stretched out in the back of my car, with his wife Linda riding in front—told me that everything about you lies in the opaque black coding bar on the back of your driver's license. Ken was not an intense conspiracy theorist; he'd come to Rachel for the job, not to follow UFOs. But this made sense to him, something of interest to chat about. I'd heard suspicious talk about driver's licenses before, from antigovernment conspiracy theorists and fundamentalist Christians.

I had stopped in Hillview on my way to Rachel, and Emmalyn, no longer the leader of the UFO Experiencers Support Group, had showed me a videotape made by Alex Jones, a Texas radio show host with a conspiratorial vision. Emmalyn had sent it along with me, to give to the people at the Little A'Le'Inn, whom she felt would identify with it as she did. Emmalyn and I watched the tape together in her Airstream trailer near the outskirts of town. She dragged intensely on her cigarettes as she took in Jones's message for the umpteenth time. In one segment, Alex Jones could be seen protesting the new procedure of *thumbprinting* at a Department of Motor Vehicles. *They* want to register you through the body now—not just to leave their mark on you, as is promised in the book of Revelation, but to capture the mark of your own physical individuation, to track you with your own embodied trace. Links from Alex Jones's website, it turned out, led to a whole slew of antilicensing outrage. A Christian family in Alabama was suing the state for demanding that licensing of drivers be accompanied by Social Security numbers. The biblical mark of the beast was recast in the ordinary procedures of state bureaucracy; in its tracking and surveillance the state was becoming profanely omnipotent, displacing the awesome power of God with the power of computers.

The encroaching pervasiveness of Social Security numbers, long felt to be part of Satan's plan by some apocalyptic Christians, grows intensified as it appears to be mandated in more and more venues. A sample letter to the government in the movement to "Resist Enumeration" argues:

> More and more people are beginning to ask why—why does the government need all this personal information linked to my SSN? And why am I being pressured into getting a social security number for my children?
>
> The Bible provides answers to these questions, along with instruction on how we should respond to the ever increasing demands for citizens to be numbered. God's People are admonished, by clearly stated example, to resist being numbered by government.
>
> We're told that King David wanted to "know the number of the People" under his authority (2 Samuel 24:2). And, Satan caused David to number all Israel (1 Chronicles 21:1). God's Word further states that David's command to number Israel "was evil in the sight of God" (1 Chronicles 21:7). Because of the People's acquiescence to the king's enumeration plan, God sent a plague upon the people (1 Chronicles 21:14). The "People" are now, once again facing new demands from the modern day "kings" to be numbered and registered. And again it is the responsibility and duty of the people to resist; regardless of how powerful or godly the particular ruling authority claims (or appears) to be, and regardless of the sincerity of their justifications. For, it is the people that will be held accountable if they do not resist. (http://www.networkusa.org/fingerprint/page6/fp-resist.html)

Here the emphasis on the word "people" foregrounds iconicities between two fundamentalist texts, the Bible and the Constitution. Just as the power of the state tries to usurp the power of God, the power of a monarch-like computerized system usurps the power of democracy: *The "People" are now again facing new demands from the modern day "kings."* And Emmalyn, who grew up in a strict Christian home, no longer went to church, but at this point she religiously attended a Constitutional Study Group to track the encroachments of these powers that be.

This resemblance between biblical and constitutional narratives against the surveillance of "kings" is not interpreted historically (that is, it does not discuss the biblical background of the writers of the Constitution). Rather the paradigmatic, simultaneous, axis is foregrounded.

And so the resemblance becomes not historical but poetic. A structure is felt to lurk below the surface of such resemblances, and just barely visible, its glimmer becomes uncanny. The parallelism between signs becomes yet another sign, pointing to a referent too large and pervasive to fully grasp.

But you don't need a Christian paradigm (nor any explicit ideology) to identify with such feelings. Rather you need a specific orientation toward power, an inchoate sense of your own distance from its invisible source, and a feeling of things slipping away into vast computerized networks (see also Dean 1998). The prophecy nods to a felt sense of our world being changed into another world, transformed by rushing technological advances in surveillance. This feeling acquires apocalyptic weight and biblical grounding.

Now, as we sped along the empty desert highway, Ken took my license again and examined it. The thin magnetic strip, I noticed, actually resembled the redacted, blacked-out segments of documents released grudgingly by the government, in UFO-related documents secured through the Freedom of Information Act. The horizontal shape of the strip suggested a line of writing "inside" or "beneath" it.

Ken said: "*They got everything in there*—when you were *born*, what you did in the *military*, where you *lived*, what *crimes* you done . . . just . . . everything!" But such items can never add up to "everything" about the phenomenological self. The flat list was deepened for Ken by the immense single metafact that *they know*.

And Ken said: "Yeah, they got a whole information system up there watching you, from the sky." This was not a discussion about the invisible corporate collection of online consumer information that would emerge a few years later, or the government surveillance of cell phones. But years before this public discourse, people *just knew*. What they said then was not in mainstream public culture, but they marked a preexisting resonance about knowledge and power, a world where Foucault's sense of the order of things would be able to slide without cognitive rupture into the next century's consumer profiling and Internet cookies.

It was two weeks after I'd taken Tina to take the test for her license. Now I was taking Linda for hers. Our car was the only one making its way through the desert, through federal-owned ranch land and the invisible borders of military property. We craned our necks to watch F-16s swoop in formation in the sky just south of the road, then stopped the car to blow the horn at meandering cows. Linda, Ken, and I looked futilely for Tina now as we drove along same route she'd come before. We knew she was parked illegally somewhere out here in the scrubby desert, living without running water or any way to get more, vulnerable to anyone who came along, just for access to the DMV and its free test.

Linda, my current passenger, had been licensed at one time, unlike Tina. Linda had gotten into some bureaucratic tangles when she moved between states. In her forties, Linda had a gaunt face that seemed older. She had come to Rachel to start over from a life that was going the wrong way in Las Vegas. When Pat came to the Salvation Army there to look for new workers, it was a stroke of fortune, though not the kind people hope for in Vegas. But Linda said without it, she'd be dead. She couldn't have survived Vegas much longer.

Once things had been different. She had built a decent working life, modest but respectable, and based on hard work and skill. She'd been a waitress for a decade in one of the superclean and regular chains that thread across the United States. At the little desert café in Rachel, waitressing with quick movements and forearm-stacked dishes, Linda spoke of her years before, working at a Pie Hut in city, as a marker of professionalism, and more, of a different orientation to the world before things had slipped out of control.

She said: *We went to Vegas on a dream.* Like many who flood into that city, they wanted not just to get rich, but to start over. When they got there though, nothing worked out the way they planned. They gambled and partied, giddy with the carnival of possibility after years of the military and solid, decent work that never quite goes anywhere. The foundation of working-class life seemed to slide out from beneath them before they realized what was happening. In her final weeks in Vegas, Linda was sleeping under a bridge.

Ken was also here from Las Vegas. He was a bit younger, a handsome African American man with a distant smile. Often I wondered what Ken thought when the bar at the café was full of the local white rural men, the cowboys and farmworkers, and the drinkers who sometimes made racist jokes as if he weren't there. Ken's friend Alex, a Desert Storm veteran who worked as a cook in the café, sometimes sat on the steps of my trailer and reminisced about life back home. He sang an old hymn he'd learned from their grandmother, one I'd heard from UFO believers in Hillview: *The earth is not my home, I'm just a-passin' through . . .* But often it was Ken, not Alex, who really seemed to me to be just passing through. In Rachel he affected a mood so impenetrably affable that it seemed he was reserving his real opinions for a less unreal place.

Today in my car, musing about the magnetic strip on the driver license, Ken seemed happy. It was good to get away even just for a half-day's trip to the Tonopah DMV. A month earlier, another friend of theirs in Rachel had been wrongly charged with driving a stolen car—it wasn't stolen, in fact, but the person who sold it to him hadn't bothered to change the tags. Now the three of them had no legal car, no way to go anywhere unless someone else would drive them the two hundred miles to Vegas on their day off. And it was clear, though they never said so, that a black man driving an unofficially tagged car would certainly be stopped in rural Nevada. Last time they had a day off and bummed a ride to Vegas, Ken and Linda had come back depressed; without a car they didn't know what to do and sat the whole time staring at the cinderblock walls of their cheap motel room.

But life in rural Nevada was a new frontier and they were again starting over. The three from Vegas were anxious to fix things up, to become legal. They were all living in a trailer a few steps from the café, had fixed it up *real nice* with plants and decorations, and adopted a puppy from the Travises' latest litter. Unlike the intoxicating possibility of Vegas, *starting over* in Rachel was overlaid with the historical narrative of a stark and sober pioneer story. Ken and Linda were clean—don't even *want* drugs here, said Linda—the desert itself was "like a rehab center." Here, she said you take responsibility for yourself. You work all day and you're too tired to party afterward, and you have to be at the café at 8:00 a.m. Yes, the café workers would drink after shift, and maybe drive on out to the black mailbox, hopping into a car with some young tourists . . . and sometimes Billy was late to work with a hangover, but he kept trying to get back on track. For all the workers trying to start over after an abject turn in Vegas, a "rehab" discourse mingled with an imagined pioneer discourse. Their conflation created the promise of a new frontier for the self.

The up-from-Vegas workers saw themselves differently here, and shyly, on this road trip to get licensed, Linda and Ken told me their new dream. They had drifted long enough; they would settle and live here. They would save up their wages and tips. With hard work and time, they would buy land across the Extraterrestrial Highway from the Little A'Le'Inn; and on their land they would build a UFO-themed miniature golf course. They had planned it all—*the tourists drive up and have nothing to do after eating an alien burger; well now they can come play UFO putt-putt golf.* Ken and Linda would be their own bosses, they would own land. Relatives would loan them the money. It would be an investment. They would make good on it and settle down.

This didn't happen. For various reasons, after a while, the lot of them left Rachel. A year later, the people I spoke with at the café did not know where they were.

But that day, Linda entered the frosty, gleaming office of the DMV. Though there was never a line, never more than one or two people in the place, you had to make an appointment a week in advance—an empty gesture of bureaucratic rationalization that made Rachel people smirk. And that day Linda smoothly passed her driver's test. Afterward we went to Burger King to celebrate Linda's new license. They insisted on buying me lunch. She had passed back into the license of the state.

Then, driving through the hard-bitten military base town of To-nopah, with its dusty hills and severe-looking casinos, something happened to dampen Linda's accomplishment. Our car was pulled over by a police officer. He had, I think, done a double-take at a black man driving in the deeply rural West with two white women. The cop vaguely hinted at a driving infraction, but didn't even bother to issue a false ticket. He just wanted to know why we were driving in his town. He manipulated a heavy silence. And when he saw that my driver's license and my plates were from different states, he looked baffled. I'd never bothered to get a new license after I'd moved to New York City from Hillview, and I had never worried about it. I realized I, too, had been skating around the edges of the license. As he stared ominously at my mugshot-like photo, I could feel us bluffing and dueling, him flashing the power of the state and me flaunting the disregard for minutiae that indexed my own middle-class ease, two small expressions of the powers that be. But he did not care about those subtle signs of habitus that I felt awarded me power over procedures of a license. In his eyes I saw us all as a motley bunch at his mercy. It was tense until he decided to just let us go.

I was relieved to get away. But an uneasy feeling subdued us. I was angry; it was so clearly a racist harassment. Ken and Linda dreamed out the windows as we sped past the Tonopah Test Range, with its 1950s-looking rocket at the fence. The setting sun turned the desert copper colors. Ken slept and Linda told me about her life, repeated her wait-ressing résumé, her history of moving around the country with a military dad. They had lived here, and here, and here. *You know I come from a good family*, she said.

Two hours after we'd been stopped by the police officer, Linda, Ken, and I descended the last hill to see Rachel, ten more miles down the road in the valley below, a tiny encampment that from here looked both staunch and vulnerable in the nothingness of the desert. That's when Linda spotted the UFO. It was hovering on the coppery mountain to the north, a blinking and unnatural glitter, like a mirror tilted to signal us. *Wake up, Ken*, she said. *That's a UFO, there it is.* Ken and Linda watched it with attentive acceptance. *Yeah—that's* something. As we neared, the thing seemed to grow, becoming more metallic and gleaming more brightly with each mile.

*There's nothing up there usually*, Linda said. *I've come this way before, there's nothing. It's just the mountain. That is a UFO.* I couldn't argue—I too had come this way many times, and had never seen anything like this on the mountain. A few miles later, the bright growing gleam disappeared as if a switch had been thrown. An unsettled feeling of the uncanny was palpable, specific as scent.

We had sped out of the world of ordinary power, away from the downpull of racist cops and frosty DMV offices. Now power was emanating instead from Area 51, the awesome center of inscrutable omnipotence, the place where the magic of the state gets infused with the supernatural. The cop's small, homely injury of the hour before evaporated in this shift to imagination. Yet this unidentified shining object was not wholly shocking. The mystery of its power was still inside the experienced fabric of things.

Did Ken and Linda think this UFO was an alien spaceship or a top-secret military experiment? As usual, it did not seem to matter. What resonated was the very *fact of power*—its vastness, its hidden sources, and its just-visible clues. What mattered was its potential for transformation, and the strange pleasure of tearing holes in the real. In the café, Linda and Ken told everyone about the UFO, how it had glittered and then *just like that* disappeared. They didn't mention the cop.

Later I talked to an old rancher who laughed at the UFO idea, teased me about it with his dead-serious, western style of teasing, and finally said we'd seen the sunset reflection of some metallic piece from the old ghost mine up on Tempiute mountain. But that, I thought, was uncanny too. The old mine was the trace of other dreams before Tina's or Ken and Linda's, where other pioneers had come to dig for prospects, to wreck their bodies, to die or move on. A few old miners still lived in Rachel, struggling with state and corporate agencies for a few dollars, requesting their due compensation for busted up backs and lungs, sick and tired of all *the forms*.

*   .   *

I have spent much of this book telling overlapping stories from a wide range of sources. At this point, finally, I want to be explicit: I have not attempted to define or analyze the social categories of the people I describe here, because there isn't one. I have taken stories, memories, and dreams from wealthy doctors and homeless drifters, men and women, young and old. A great many of the people here have experienced shifts in their economic position; they grew up poor and became a comfortable small business owner, or they fell from the middle class into a period of economic anxiety. Most, but not all, of the people represented here are white. But using social categories to analyze things like class position, here, would mislead from what I'm trying to say about the unfinalized structures of feeling and imagination that emerge in uncanny talk. These stories are memories and fragments that belong not to a single social position; rather they flood into and out of intersubjective spaces, and in doing so they express something about history and power. Memory and fantasy, like injury, exceed individual experience and become social, lingering and changing. My argument, in the end, is that what we need to know can be heard in the poetic resonance of these stories from multiple sources.

The narrative effect performs an ethnographic observation that saturates every story here: that vernacular theories of power and captivity in America often work through cultivating apophenia into a deep sense of resonance. This is how many people make their poetic, epistemological, and social worlds: by tuning in to the half-rhyme, the near correlation, the parallel tropes that intimate a pattern. And then, in metatalk about that pattern, you spin it back out again into the world to meet up with another story, to make another rhyme. It makes sense, and remains mysterious at the same time. This effect produces rushes of feeling, like the "static state filled with vibratory motion or resonance" that pulses suddenly in ordinary unspoken moments (Stewart 2007). Like an art object, a sense of wonder resonates out from the story itself, moving beyond its borders; "for resonance, like nostalgia, is impure, a hybrid forged in . . . barely acknowledged gaps" (Greenblatt 1990: 27). Here, in many social worlds where people talk about UFOs and all the weird stuff that happens in the world, resonance is the subject matter. It is the way things work deep down, below the appearance of the random, the contingent, the meaningless. Seeing and naming inexplicable parallels between things is a way to articulate hard-to-name structures of feeling. They become artful and meaningful through narrative and poetic utterances.

More important, I have used the uncanny in its most deeply social register, attempting to present a real discursive, affective, and poetic process in America, one that is ethnographically describable. The uncanny suggests, here, an ambivalent desire for a redemptive citizenship in America along with an inchoate sense of nostalgia and loss. Numerous anthropologists and other scholars of social life have for decades found in the uncanny a productive way to describe real, unfinalized coconstructions of modernity and nostalgia, and global and local configurations, as they are performed in popular imaginaries and material shifts.

Sometimes conspiracy theories begin to make sense beyond that "outsider-y" (Dean 2009) soil that cultivates them. Things first look like weeds when they begin to push their way up in cracks and untended spaces. But the roots are deep. Years after the towers fell, a multilayered feeling grows and spreads more widely in public culture—a sense that there is more to the operations of power than people might know, that government surveillance, technological surveillance, and corporate surveillance might converge in ways that seem intertwined, confusing, outrageous. On one level a growing mistrust of surveillance occurs over publicly debated news events, focusing on current revelations from an empire still at war against a shifting terror. And on another level, there filters in a whole other set of memories and partly acknowledged suspicions that have been drifting underneath the clearly lit public sphere, underneath things all along. The ghosts are real here too, as are the prophecies. Discourses that seemed completely marginal ten years ago now begin to echo at the center of things; the familiar and the unfamiliar, as always in the uncanny, begin to converge

I have tried in these pages to show how America is still haunted by its own historical crimes and wounds. Ghosts always haunt us with the historical injustices of the past; their uncanny presences hold open social memories that seep into the present and disrupt its attempts at narrative closure. The uncanny denaturalizes the familiar, until the strange and the frightening lead back to what we already know, to what was meant to be completely forgotten. This is the social work ghosts do, rattling the chains of historical traumas that won't remain buried (Derrida 1994; Gordon 1997; Ivy 1995; Morrison 1988; Pemberton 1994; Mueggler 2001). But in late twentieth (and early twenty-first century) America, the ghost of memory often haunts through the *futuristic* figure of a UFO.

But this is how culture moves ahead in its ordinary registers too—histories coiling into futures, the compelling newness of things authorized and deepened by repeating—faintly, distortedly—what has come before. To catch us up with its rush of the new, the alien contains within it something that crossed a more familiar space, something we half-know. As Greg Urban maps out the force of accelerative culture, "The force behind . . . accelerative culture is the interest it generates, which stems in part from its novelty" (Urban 2001: 16). But the new catches our interest through its "resembling something from the past that has already generated interest," though the "resemblances . . . are not (or not necessarily) blatant" (Urban 2001: 16). Subtle resemblance in the sense of acceleration and nostalgia here makes a resonance of the real.

Anna Tsing wrote almost two decades ago about people living in "out of the way" places: "My sense is that there is always an uncanny magic involved in imagining . . . the beleaguered community in the heart of the oppressive system. . . . It is a magic that allows groups defined by externally imposed categories of cultural difference simultaneously to resent and to embrace those categories" (1994: 280).

My object of ethnographic inquiry, then, has not been Indian captivity narratives or UFO abduction narratives. It is not a single specific performance or place. Still, as in a more traditional ethnography, the object here is still something that I observed, and have also participated in making. As Debbora Battaglia (2012) has observed in a very different context, we can find artfulness in utterances that are not intended to be art, especially "when description is congruent with the strange reality it seeks to relate, when it iterates as . . . 'defamiliarization' or 'enstrangement'" (Battaglia 2012: 1093).[2] Like most art forms, here it is expressive, and it produces feeling, sociability, meaning, and an embodied, patterned sense of aesthetic rightness, and a kind of "groove" (Feld 1995). It creates a feeling of pattern and structure, the way "the reiterative figure of sound" does for Jakobson's poetic function of language (1960). The "reiterative figure" here is not sound per se but rather image, trope, or theme. And so the ethnographic object, here, has not been a single story, myth, or poem form. Instead it has been the intertextual, poetic process of how people recognize the resemblances and patterns between events and stories, and how they use that chime to cast a new story about powers that seems too big to name. The reiterative figure produces and reproduces a sense of resonance that exceeds whatever is there. And in the impact of these resonant chimes that people feel, they say: the weird stuff is out there, the weird stuff makes things seem to come together but never be a final story.

The uncanny carries a sense of the liminal, not as a transition in a linear progression to a new reintegrated state but rather as particular "structure of feeling" (Williams 1977). But while the uncanny is experienced as something "lodged between" the spaces of code, it is also completely saturated by "the rules of law," not outside them. But in the light of an uncanny space, naturalized rules *almost* appear to be what they are—rules, conventions, constructions. As Turner (1979, 1981) wrote of the liminal (and also of the "liminoid" [1981], its more naturalized form) this space breaks down code into its parts. The parts loom out of order and become grotesque. They acquire the horror of taboo in Mary Douglas's (1966) classic sense of the term—things out of place that threaten a naturalized order. Douglas recognized that such ambiguity is not only the basis of taboo but also of creativity; "the richness of poetry depends on [it] . . . aesthetic pleasure arises from the perceiving of inarticulate forms" (37).

In the uncanny, the naturalized "indicative mood" of the ordinary grows contingent with its own "subjunctive" latent critique.[3] Things as they are indicated in naturalized terms threaten to fall apart. Like poetry, they are glimpsed in their constitutive parts, often through repetition, or the intensification of tropes. But if they were to appear fully as conventions, they would no longer be uncanny. Their double-voicing through repetition and parallelism would be fully consciously crafted, politically rich, poetic critiques, rising out of a consciously artful and participatory social identity, speaking in its relation to a dominant other. But in the double-voiced, poetic decomposition of the uncanny, such critical denaturalization isn't ever fully complete. It remains half articulated, a kind of "partial knowledge" (Petryna 2002).

In many times and places, uncanny repetitions, and the hauntings of a before, can speak both to the colonizing imagination and to the experience of those whose labor fuels it. Keeping us alert to the potential for the accidental, and to the uneasiness of recognizing a native mind whose differences might not be different enough, these repetitions disrupt the dream of a smoothly safe modernity with "the abruptly reawakened memory of forgotten danger . . . the uncanny sensation of something known all along but routinely suppressed" (Pemberton 2003: 85). And UFO discourse performs the middle of a long, troubled American story of conquest, a shifting, unstable desire trying to construct and express a different point of identification—one that just doesn't feel at one with the order of the world as it is. The weird, overdetermined feeling here can give us insight into other contingent American desires, a projected longing for a *something* that is not fulfilled. This desire can wind up taking multiple directions in affects surrounding encounters with power, from right-wing, antigovernment conspiracy to the liberatory; it wants to live on the other side, whatever that is, and hopes there is some different kind of force lurking there, beyond the ache of any ordinary life made captive by powers that always seem too overwhelming to pin down to a single story.

# Coda

## *One More Thing*

I'll end again with a final story. One day I spent many hours talking to a UFO believer who rattled me. I had started out with my sense of things intact. I was cheerful and curious, but he talked and talked for hours about the government and aliens, insinuating threats and sinister dangers until my eyes began to dim. I had to fly home as soon as we had finished talking, and I drove through the desert numbly, his words stuck in my hair, his sinister predictions still thickening around me in the car.

My flight left at midnight. I arrived in the city hours early and aimlessly drove the streets. I'd spent some time in Vegas before this. Then the city was a glorious riot, dazzlingly surreal and banal in strobing alteration, a comic festival of simulacra. Not now. The frantic lights shocked my system.

And then, waiting to board my plane, I was approached by a Man in Black. At first I did not realize, despite his dapper and telltale black suit, who had come to sit beside me. It happened so fast. He began to converse in a clipped accent. He was very short and sported a jaunty mustache. He showed me a profusion of colorful folders from his Business Seminar. They were so shiny and had so many pie charts. He had been here for the edification and promotion of vitamins that counteracted obesity. He had perhaps not made a great deal of sales, but he had certainly facilitated many situations.

He asked my name and I told him. He asked where I lived and I told him. He asked what I did and I said I was a writer. He asked what I wrote, and I said I was tired now, and it was nothing personal but I was going to read.

Ah! Susan! he said. I see you have in you *the sociological imagination!* Very good, very good. You have a lot on your mind. I will not occupy you.

He took my hand, and squeezed it very hard, and looked at me significantly; and then he walked into the crowd, and evaporated.

It was then I thought he was a Man in Black. He'd said . . . sociological imagination! He was telling me he knew who I was. How often had I read of this, heard it and tape-recorded it as folklore? Encountering a Man in Black is always a bizarre and inexplicable encounter. It is uncanny in the classic sense; some think the strange men are automatons.

At midnight we boarded the plane. The mood on board was muted, a pensive feel of lost money, with people dreaming out the windows—a far cry from the reveling camaraderie in anticipation of jackpots on the flight from New York to Vegas. This was the downward turn of that wheel. The plane climbed. People slept and murmured to their children. My body was exhausted and rigid with the day. Over the fasten seatbelt lights, multiple silent John Travoltas were blasted by otherworldly beams of light. Conspiracies snaked through my blood, touched forgotten images, and linked together in a chain of unstoppable increase.

What is down there? a child asked behind me. That is the earth, her mother said. It was raining on the window. The vanishing ground was black with quickly changing patterns of light. Inside, we passengers breathed each other's exhalations. Like the stories we told, we somehow made them our own breath. Our invisible contagions seeped into the cabin, entered each other's bodies, and began to culture there. The rain on the window recycled from a time we can't remember, and our memories are not simply our own.

# Notes

## Chapter 1

1. See Jodi Dean's (2009) cogent analysis of how the failures of the Left in the 1990s led to the development of the contemporary engulfment of democracy by neoliberalism.

2. Hillview is a fictitious name of the city where these events occur. Throughout this book, I use fictitious names and some altered details to protect the privacy of the people who appear here. People who have become well known in popular venues beyond this book (those who have appeared in various media, for example) are usually called by their real names.

3. This kind of thinking through apophenia as a channel into the paranormal was pioneered by the maverick philosopher of the uncanny, Charles Fort (1974), who remains a venerated figure for those who explore "the weird stuff," as I will call it later. His *Book of the Damned* treats flying saucers as part of a range of material excluded from scientific inquiry. On a vernacular level, see thefortean-times.com; for a masterfully engaging study of Fort, see Kripal 2011.

4. The abductor is omniscient, and people explicitly link the abducting alien omniscience to the gaze of evil human doctors and to the therapists who peer into abductees' minds to hypnotize them (Lepselter 1994; Brown 2007). The alien "has an air of authority . . . his is clinical and brusque . . . abductees sometimes call him doctor because of his demeanor and his task" (Jacobs 1992: 97). This "Taller Being" performs "mindscan," which "entails a deep penetrating staring into the abductees eyes" (Jacob 1992: 97).

5. See Dean (2003) for a critique of Mack's conflation of abduction experience with other world spiritual experiences; also Battaglia (2005) on Mack, and on Dean's critique.

6. Walton 1978.

7. The Schwa company was started in 1992 by Bill Barker, who in a 1998 interview with *Wired* magazine described his dissemination of the alien logo as "a symbol of our future—a mirror looking into what we're becoming—technological, maybe." But this was not the earnest message about meaning and transformation that most Hillview UFO believers craved; rather the Schwa company saw the inexplicable appearance of alien signs as "a satire of postmodern life and advertising . . . an experiment in cultural design" in a small business. By the time of the interview in 1998, his images had been sold to AOL for gaming; the article declared that "with Pyramid's (the multi-player game) appearance on America Online, Schwa has found its first truly mainstream distribution outlet" (Brown 1998); Barker said he was hoping for "a mini-phenomenon" (Brown 1998) as the figures grew in popularity.

8. Other studies have built on Hufford's in culturally specific ways; for example the medical anthropologist Shelley Adler (2010) described how a chest-crushing nocturnal spirit killed Hmong immigrant men who were living liminal lives in the United States.

9. As Kathleen Stewart has described her own ethnography, my style here "at times . . . performs a sharp disjuncture between discourses—mine and theirs . . . at other times it attempts a hybridization" (1996: 40).

10. I retain certain (but not all) conventions traditionally used in ethnopoetic transcriptions of oral performances. When I transcribe direct oral narratives in clearly bounded stories, I use small capitals to signify a performatively louder voice. I use *italics* to indicate a focused, intensified pronunciation (cf. Tedlock 1992). I also use *italics* throughout my text to indicate my own intensified voice. This occurs in my performative use of double-voiced or reported speech when I want to signify that indicating a direct quotation would be inappropriate, for example, because the double voice occurs through re-entextualizing a phrase, or re-iterating a specific word that I heard in another context. My use of italics within my own text (as opposed to within a clearly marked oral story) is a way of some-times blurring the boundaries between my own voice and that of my subjects, calling attention to the performative quality of both our texts. This is also a way of attending to meaning beyond the referent, foregrounding the sound and feel of the talk I want to describe. I do not always use quotations for this kind of reported speech because I sometimes intend to close the distance between my own voice and that of others in cocreating theory and story.

11. What Masco calls "the nuclear uncanny" is an anxious "perceptual space caught between apocalyptic expectation and sensory fulfillment, a psychic effect produced, on the one hand, by living within the temporal ellipsis separating a nuclear attack and the actual end of the world, and on the other, by inhabiting an environmental space threatened by military industrial radiation" (Masco 2006: 27). Its changes range from biological mutations to "new social formations brought together by the joint experience of risk and/or fear of contamination" (27). And the new social formations he is referring to, formations that emerged within the ubiquitous effects of nuclear anxiety (including peace activists, uranium min-ers, and indigenous victims of testing [Masco 2006: 343], further produce dis-courses and social feelings; the direct responses to nuclear anxieties break down in unpredictable half-lives, linking up with other affective domains.


Chapter 2

1. Hillview is a fictitious name of the city where these events occur. Throughout this book, I use fictitious names and altered details to protect the privacy of the people who appear here. People who have become well known in popular venues beyond this book (those who have appeared in various media, for example) may be called by their real names.

2. Freud (1963) writes that the *unheimlich* (the uncanny) partially reveals something disturbingly familiar or "homey" (*heimlich*). Tracing the history of the two words, Freud finds that among its shades of meaning, *heimlich* (homey, famil-iar) sometimes means its opposite, *unheimlich*: "What is *heimlich* thus comes to be *unheimlich* . . . *heimlich* is not unambiguous . . . on the one hand it means that which is familiar and congenial and on the other, that which is concealed and kept out of sight. . . . Thus *heimlich* is a word the meaning of which develops towards an ambivalence until it finally coincides with its opposite, *unheimlich* (375–77).

3. Psychology-based trauma theory takes it as a given that experiences of forced immobilization and dissociative memory—or trance memory—go hand in hand. In standard psychology of trauma, dissociative kinds of memory occur when trauma is accompanied by physical or emotional paralysis, the sense that there is

*nothing you can do* (Herman 1977). Traumatic constriction can be forced by the perpetrator. Or it can be a shocked response to the overwhelming sensation of helplessness in the moment of violence, the paralysis of terror.

4. Art Bell's *Coast to Coast*, a popular overnight radio show focusing on the paranormal. Except for occasional appearances Art Bell retired from the show in 2007.

## Chapter 3

1. Thousands of captivity narratives have circulated over the course of Euro-American colonization; the popular narrative of Mary Rowlandson was our nation's first bestseller (Derounian-Stodola 1999). Over the past few decades, many scholars have elaborated on the polyvalent significance of the genre and its importance to the construction of American national identity, from stories of colonial contact to kidnappings of the twenty-first century. As Ebersole (1995: 2) writes, "Since the seventeenth century, tales of captivity have been used in the Euro-American world in diverse ways as vehicle for reflection on larger social, religious and ideological issues." Severance notes that captivity on the frontier was so common that news reports of Indian abduction "occasioned little if any further commentary in the press" (quoted in Ebersole 1995: 6). However, the narrative following the captives' release was eagerly awaited, often going through multiple editions over many years (6).

2. Of course, some captivity narratives did not "end" with the captive's return or even with her or his death; most famously, perhaps, Mary Jemison, captured by the Seneca in the eighteenth century, eventually was given the opportunity to return home but chose to stay with the tribe after having children with a Seneca husband, knowing that white society would reject her dark-skinned children.

3. Others have also noticed the connection between alien abduction and Indian captivity narratives. UFO abduction is mentioned by Derounian-Stodola (1999) in a list of captivity narratives types. Sturma (2002) methodically and thoroughly outlines many of the parallels between the two genres. In a beautiful article, Barbeito (2005) writes about the UFO abduction story's connection to Indian captivity, focusing especially insightfully on the trope of the body's invasion in each genre. It is, perhaps, another level of resonance that Barbeito's article appeared just months after my own dissertation; it seems each of us independently noticed uncannily parallel points of connection between many of the same UFO and Indian abduction stories. It seemed another uncanny coincidence that I read Barbeito's 2005 article connecting alien abductions and Indian captivity narratives soon after writing about it myself.

4. This account incorporates many circulating popular stories about Roswell, both written and oral, too numerous to cite. Perhaps the most popular and prolific writer on Roswell is Stanton Friedman. See Don Berliner and Stanton Friedman's 1997 *Crash at Corona: The US Military's Retrieval and Cover-up of a UFO*.

5. See especially Dean (1998) for a very incisive analysis of the idea of "the powers that be" and the problem of the real in UFO discourses.

6. http://www.youtube.com/watch?v=J6iMsfsoVG4√, accessed 2008.

7. In Mary Rowlandson's iconic Puritan Indian captivity narrative, the captive's journey with her captors becomes an allegory of her soul's progress toward greater Christian faith.

8. Although I am citing the Travis Walton website, the story (and the question about it at the UFO convention) was originally presented in his 1978 book *The Walton Experience* (and in the 1993 film made of his book, *Fire in the Sky*, a highly revised version of the story).

9. Jacobsen (2011) asserts that the Soviet project of creating human "alien" bodies followed the medical experimentation developed by Nazi scientists.

## Chapter 4

1. On TV, an alien autopsy was said to be the broadcast of a mysteriously discovered film of unknown origin or authenticity. It showed a strange body that looked almost human. Though I was prepared to see the televised alien autopsy as a stunt, it gave me a nauseous, uncanny spin. Surrounded by white- gowned pathologists in what looked like a 1950s-style dissection lab, the sad, inert, large-headed body looked like someone who had been injured by radiation. And this is indeed the theory proposed by the investigative journalist Annie Jacobson (2011), who believes that the legend of aliens comes from glimpses of real Soviet radiation experiments on people.

2. Pronounced "kai-oats"—the anglicized two-syllable pronunciation.

## Chapter 5

1. See Brown 2007 for a thorough and insightful analysis of the standard alien abduction story.

2. See Brown 2007 for further analysis of abduction imagery vis-à-vis reproductive technologies.

3. These place-names, like the names of the speakers here, have been anonymized.

4. In her work on the poetics of modernity in Japan, Marilyn Ivy (1995) makes a connection between the discursive elaboration of the hometown, and Freud's idea of the uncanny, the *unheimlich*—unhomely. When the hometown begins to fade as an unmarked place, the world of origins and of nature becomes densely imagined as both safe and terrifying, natural and strange, and filled with the returning spirits of a repressed realm of the natural.

## Chapter 6

1. In this chapter, as usual, I use real names for people who have appeared in public media, and pseudonyms for those who have not. However, I may use pseudonyms at times for public people when they are speaking of things that were not necessarily directed at a media public.

2. Battaglia writes that the different context can be found in the journals of a Soviet cosmonaut, who as an "ethnographer" of outer space describes his own experiences of defamiliarization.

3. Turner (1981) called it "the subjunctive mood" of liminality: it "is a time and place lodged between all times and spaces defined and governed . . . by the rules of law, politics and religion and by economic necessity" (Turner 1981: 161).

# Bibliography

Abzug, Robert H. 1994. *Cosmos Crumbling: American Reform and the Religious Imagination*. New York: Oxford University Press.

Adler, Shelley R. 2010. *Sleep Paralysis: Night-mares, Nocebos, and the Mind-Body Connection* (Studies in Medical Anthropology). Piskataway, NJ: Rutgers University Press.

Badmington, Neil. 2004. *Alien Chic: Posthumanism and the Other Within*. New York: Routledge.

Bakhtin, Mikhail. 1973. *Problems of Dostoevsky's Poetics*. Trans. R. W. Rotsel. Ann Arbor, MI: Ardis.

Bakhtin, Mikhail. 1981. *The Dialogic Imagination: Four Essays*. Ed. Michael Holquist. Trans. Caryl Emerson and Michael Holquist. Austin: University of Texas Press.

Barbeito, Patricia Felisa. 2005. "'He's Making Me Feel Things in My Body That I Don't Feel': The Body as Battleground in Accounts of Alien Abduction." *Journal of American Culture* 28.2: 201–15.

Battaglia, Debbora. 2005. Introduction. In *E.T. Culture: Anthropology in Outer Spaces*. Ed. Debbora Battaglia. Durham, NC: Duke University Press.

Battaglia, Debbora. 2012. "Coming In at an Unusual Angle: Exo-surprise and the Fieldworking Cosmonaut." *Anthropological Quarterly* 85.4: 1089–106.

Bauman, Richard. 2004. *A World of Others' Words: Cross-Cultural Perspectives on Intertextuality*. Malden, MA: Wiley-Blackwell.

Bauman, Richard, and Charles Briggs. 1990. "Poetics and Performance as Critical Perspectives on Language and Social Life." *Annual Review of Anthropology* 19: 59–88.

Bauman, Richard, and Charles Briggs. 1992. "Genre, Intertextuality and Social Power." *Journal of Linguistic Anthropology* 2.2: 131–72.

Benjamin, Walter. 1978. *Reflections: Essays, Aphorisms, Autobiographical Writings*. Ed. Peter Demetz. Trans. E. F. N. Jephcott. New York: Schocken.

Benjamin, Walter. 1988. *Illuminations*. Ed. Hannah Arendt. Trans. Harry Zohn. New York: Schocken.

Berlant, Lauren. 1997. *The Queen of America Goes to Washington City: Essays on Sex and Citizenship*. Durham, NC: Duke University Press.

Berlant, Lauren. 2011. *Cruel Optimism*. Durham, NC: Duke University Press.

Berliner, Don, and Stanton T. Friedman. 1997. *Crash at Corona: The U.S. Military Retrieval and Cover-up of a UFO*. New York: Marlowe.

Bourke, John G. 2003 [1892]. *Medicine Men of the Apache*. University Press of the Pacific.

Boyer, Paul. 1992. *When Time Shall Be No More: Prophecy Belief in Modern American Culture*. Cambridge, MA: Belknap Press of Harvard University Press.

Brown, Bridget. 2007. *They Know Us Better Than We Know Ourselves: The History and Politics of Alien Abduction*. New York: NYU Press.

Brown, Janelle. 1998. Aliens Land on AOL. *Wired*, February 23. On the Web: http://www.wired.com/culture/lifestyle/news/1998/02/10465.

Brown, Michael. 1997. *The Channeling Zone: American Spirituality in an Anxious Age*. Cambridge, MA: Harvard University Press.

Bullard, Thomas. 1988. "UFO Abduction Reports: The Supernatural Kidnap Narrative Returns in Technological Guise." *Journal of American Folklore* 102: 146–69.

Campbell, Glenn. 1995. *Area 51: A Viewer's Guide*. Edition 4.01. Rachel, NV: Glenn Campbell.

Campbell, Glenn. 1996. *A Short History of Rachel, Nevada*. Prepared for the Rachel Senior Center.

Caruth, Cathy, ed. 1995. *Trauma: Explorations in Memory*. Baltimore: Johns Hopkins University Press.

Castiglia, Christopher. 1996. *Bound and Determined: Captivity, Culture-Crossing, and White Womanhood from Mary Rowlandson to Patty Hearst*. Chicago: University of Chicago Press.

Clancy, Susan. 2005. *Abducted: How People Come to Believe They Were Abducted by Aliens*. Cambridge, MA: Harvard University Press.

Clancy, Susan, Richard J. McNally, Daniel L. Schacter, Mark F. Lenzenweger, and Roger K. Pitman. 2002. "Memory Distortion in People Reporting Abduction by Aliens." *Journal of Abnormal Psychology* 111.3: 455–61.

Comaroff, J., and J. L. Comaroff. 2000. "Millennial Capitalism: First Thoughts on a Second Coming." *Public Culture* 12.2: 291–343.

Corso, Philip. 1998. *The Day after Roswell*. New York: Simon and Schuster.

Csordas, Thomas. 1993. "Somatic Modes of Attention." *Cultural Anthropology* 8.2: 135–56.

Danton, Elizabeth. 2003. Introduction. *Grimm's Fairy Tales*, Jacob and Wilhelm Grimm. New York: Barnes and Noble.

Darlington, David. 1997. *Area 51: The Dreamland Chronicles*. New York: Henry Holt.

Davis, Richard [alleged]. 1995. Letter to Mr. Steven Schiff. On the Web: http://www.parascope.com/articles/1296/mj12gao.htm.

Davis, Sandra K. 1994. "Fighting over Public Lands." *Western Public Lands and Environmental Politics*, ed. Charles Davis, 11–31. Boulder, CO: Westview Press.

Dean, Jodi. 1997. "The Familiarity of Strangeness." *Theory and Event* 1.2.

Dean, Jodi. 1998. *Aliens in America*. Ithaca, NY: Cornell University Press.

Dean, Jodi. 2002. *Publicity's Secret: How Technoculture Capitalizes on Democracy*. Ithaca, NY: Cornell University Press.

Dean, Jodi. 2009. *Democracy and Other Neoliberal Fantasies: Communicative Capitalism and Left Politics*. Durham, NC: Duke University Press.

Dellamora, Richard, ed. 1995. *Postmodern Apocalypse: Theory and Practice at the End.* Philadelphia: University of Pennsylvania Press.

Derounian-Stodola, Kathryn Zabelle. 1999. Introduction. *Women's Indian Captivity Narratives,* ed. Kathryn Zabelle Derounian-Stodola. New York: Penguin.

Derrida, Jacques. 1994. *Specters of Marx: The State of the Debt, the Work of Mourning and the New International.* Trans. Peggy Kamuf. New York: Routledge.

Dorson, Richard M. 1950. *America Begins: Early American Writing.* New York: Pantheon.

Douglas, Mary. 1966. *Purity and Danger: An Analysis of the Concepts of Pollution and Taboo.* London: Routledge and Kegan Paul.

Ebersole, Gary L. 1995. *Captured by Texts: Puritan to Postmodern Images of Indian Captivity.* Charlottesville: University Press of Virginia.

Faludi, Susan. 2007. *The Terror Dream: Myth and Misogyny in an Insecure America.* New York: Picador.

Fassin, Didier, and Richard Rechtman. *The Empire of Trauma: An Inquiry into the Condition of Victimhood.* Princeton, NJ: Princeton University Press.

Feld, Steven. 1994. "Aesthetics of Iconicity of Style, or 'Lift-up-over Sounding:' Getting into the Kaluli Groove." *Music Grooves,* Charles Keil and Steven Feld, 109–50. Chicago: University of Chicago Press.

Feld, Steven. 2012. *Jazz Cosmopolitanism in Accra: Five Musical Years in Ghana.* Durham, NC: Duke University Press.

Feld, Steven, and Keith Basso, eds. 1996. *Senses of Place.* Santa Fe: School of American Research Press.

Fort, Charles. 1974. *The Complete Books of Charles Fort.* New York: Dover Press.

Foucault, Michel. 1979. *Discipline and Punish: The Birth of the Prison.* Trans. Alan Sheridan. New York: Vintage.

Foucault, Michel. 1989. *The Birth of the Clinic.* Trans. A. M. Sheridan Smith. New York: Routledge.

Freud, Sigmund. 1956 [1915]. "Repression." *Collected Papers,* vol. 4, trans. Joan Riviere. London: Hogarth Press.

Freud, Sigmund. 1963 [1919]. "The Uncanny." *Studies in Parapsychology,* ed. Philip Rieff, 19–60. New York: Macmillan.

Gordon, Avery. 1997. *Ghostly Matters: Haunting and the Sociological Imagination.* Minneapolis: University of Minnesota Press.

Greenblatt, Stephen. 1990. "Resonance and Wonder." *Bulletin of the American Academy of Arts and Sciences* 43.4: 11–34.

Grosz, Elizabeth. 1994. *Volatile Bodies: Towards a Corporeal Feminism.* Bloomington: Indiana University Press.

Harding, Susan Friend. 1987. "Convicted by the Holy Spirit: The Rhetoric of Fundamental Baptist Conversion." *American Ethnologist* 14: 167–80.

Harding, Susan Friend. 2000. *The Book of Jerry Falwell: Fundamentalist Language and Politics.* Princeton, NJ: Princeton University Press.

Herman, Judith Lewis. *Trauma and Recovery: The Aftermath of Violence—from Domestic Abuse to Political Terror.* New York: Basic Books, HarperCollins.

Hopkins, Bud. 1981. *Missing Time*. New York: Ballantine.

Hopkins, Bud. 1987. *Intruders*. New York: Ballantine.

Hufford, David. 1982. *The Terror That Comes in the Night: An Experience-Centered Study of Supernatural Assault Traditions*. Philadelphia: University of Pennsylvania Press.

Ivy, Marilyn. 1995. *Discourses of the Vanishing: Modernity, Phantasm, Japan*. Chicago: University of Chicago Press.

Jacobs, David. 1992. *Secret Life: Firsthand Accounts of UFO Abductions*. New York: Simon and Shuster.

Jakobson, Roman. 1960. "Concluding Statement: Linguistics and Poetics." *Style and Language*, ed. T. A. Sebeok, 35–377. Cambridge: MIT Press.

Jameson, Fredric. 1981. *The Political Unconscious: Narrative as a Socially Symbolic Act*. Ithaca, NY: Cornell University Press.

Kapchan, Deborah. 2007. *Traveling Spirit Masters: Moroccan Gnawa Trance and Music in the Global Marketplace*. Middletown, CT: Wesleyan University Press.

Keil, Charles, and Steven Feld. 1994. *Music Grooves*. Chicago: University of Chicago Press.

Kelly, Fanny. 1990. *Narrative of My Captivity among the Sioux Indians*. Ed. Clark C. Spence and Mary Lee Spence. Chicago: Lakeside Press.

Kolodny, Annette. 1984. *The Land Before Her: Fantasy and Experience of the American Frontiers, 1630–1860*. Chapel Hill: University of North Carolina Press.

Kripal, Jeffrey J. 2011. *Mutants and Mystics: Science Fiction, Superhero Comics and the Paranormal*. Chicago: University of Chicago Press.

Kristeva, Julia. 1982. *Powers of Horror: An Essay on Abjection*. Trans. Leon S. Roudiez. New York: Columbia University Press.

Lawhon, Loy. 2000. "Betty and Barney." On the Web: http://ufos.about.com/library/weekly/aa051500a.htm.

Leiby, Richard. 1997. "Secrets under the Sun." *Washington Post*, July 20. On the Web: http://www.ufomind.com/area51/articles/1997/washpost_970720.html.

Lepselter, Susan. 1997. "From the Earth Native's Point of View: The Earth, the Extraterrestrial and the Natural Ground of Home." *Public Culture* 9: 197–208.

Lévi-Strauss, Claude. 1966. *The Savage Mind*. London: Weidenfeld and Nicolson; Chicago: University of Chicago Press.

Lewis, James R., ed. 1995. *The Gods Have Landed: New Religions from Other Worlds*. Albany: SUNY Press.

Masco, Joseph. 2006. *The Nuclear Borderlands: The Manhattan Project in Post–Cold War New Mexico*. Princeton, NJ: Princeton University Press.

Menkin, Michael. 2003. "Stop Alien Abductions." On the Web: http://www.stopabductions.com/Bio.htm, accessed January 2013.

Morrison, Toni. 1998. *Beloved*. New York: Columbia University Press.

Mueggler, Erik. 2001. *The Age of Wild Ghosts: Memory, Violence, and Place in Southwest China*. Berkeley: University of California Press.

O'Leary, Stephen D. 1994. *Arguing the Apocalypse: A Theory of Millennial Rhetoric*. New York: Oxford University Press.

Orr, Jackie. *The Panic Diaries: A Geneology of Panic Disorder*. Durham, NC: Duke University Press.

Patton, Phil. 1998. *Dreamland: Travels inside the Secret World of Roswell and Area 51*. New York: Villard Books.

Pemberton, John. 1994. *On the Subject of "Java."* Ithaca, NY: Cornell University Press.

Propp, Vladimir. 1968. *Morphology of the Folktale*. Trans. Laurence Scott. Austin: University of Texas Press.

Ramsey, Colin. 1994. "Cannibalism and Infant Killing: A System of 'Demonizing' Motifs in Indian Captivity Narratives." *Clio* 24.1: 55–68.

"Resist Enumeration." On the Web: http://www.networkusa.org/fingerprint/page6/fp- resist.html.

Robinson, J. Dennis. N.d. "The Grounding of Betty Hill." Seacoast New Hampshire.com. http://seacoastnh.com/History/As_I_Please/The_Grounding_of_Betty_Hill.

Rojcewicz, Peter. 1987. "The 'Men in Black': Experience and Tradition—Analogues with the Traditional Devil Hypothesis." *Journal of American Folklore* 100: 148–60.

Rojcewicz, Peter. 1989. "The Folklore of the 'Men in Black': A Challenge to the Prevailing Paradigm." *ReVISION*. 11.4: 5–1.

Roth, Christopher F. 2005. "Ufology as Anthropology: Race, Extraterrestrials, and the Occult." *E.T. Culture: Anthropology in Outer Spaces*, ed. Debbora Battaglia. Durham, NC: Duke University Press.

Rowlandson, Mary. 1998. "A Narrative of the Captivity and Restoration of Mrs. Mary Rowlandson." *Women's Indian Captivity Narratives*, ed. Kathryn Zabelle Derounian-Stodola. New York: Penguin.

Sanders, Todd, and Harry G. West. 2003. "Power Concealed in the New World Order." *Transparency and Conspiracy: Ethnographies of Suspicion in the New World Order*, ed. Harry G. West and Todd Sanders, 1–38. Durham, NC: Duke University Press.

Sennett, Richard, and Jonathan Cobb. 1992. *The Hidden Injuries of Class*. New York: Norton.

Slotkin, Richard. 1973. *Regeneration through Violence: The Mythology of the American Frontier, 1600–1860*. Middletown, CT: Wesleyan University Press.

Steedly, Mary. 1993. *Hanging without a Rope: Narrative Experience in Colonial and Postcolonial Karoland*. Princeton, NJ: Princeton University Press.

Stewart, Kathleen. 1991. "On the Politics of Cultural Theory: A Case for 'Contaminated' Cultural Critique." *Social Research* 58.2: 395–412.

Stewart, Kathleen. 1996. *A Space on the Side of the Road: Cultural Poetics in an "Other" America*. Princeton, NJ: Princeton University Press.

Stewart, Kathleen. 2007. *Ordinary Affects*. Durham, NC: Duke University Press.

Stewart, Susan. 1993. *On Longing: Narratives of the Miniature, the Gigantic, the Souvenir, the Collection*. Durham, NC: Duke University Press.

Stewart, Susan. 1995. "Lyric Possession." *Critical Inquiry* 22.1: 34–63.

Streiber, Whitley. 1987. *Communion: A True Story*. New York: William Morrow.

Strong, Pauline Turner. 1999. *Captive Selves, Captivating Others: The Politics and Poetics of Colonial American Captivity Narratives*. Boulder, CO: Westview Press.

Sturken, Marita. 1997. *Tangled Memories: The Vietnam War, the AIDS Epidemic, and the Politics of Remembering*. Berkeley: University of California Press.

Sturma, Michael. 2002. "Aliens and Indians: A Comparison of Abduction and Captivity Narratives. *Journal of Popular Culture* 36: 318–34.

Taussig, Michael. 1997. *The Magic of the State*. New York: Routledge.

Todorov, Tzvetan. 1975. *The Fantastic*. Ithaca, NY: Cornell University Press.

Tsing, Anna Lowenhaupt. 1994. "From the Margins." "Further Inflections: Toward Ethnographies of the Future." *Cultural Anthropology* 9.3: 279–97.

Turner, Victor. 1979 [1964]. "Betwixt and Between: The Liminal Period in Rites de Passage." *Reader in Comparative Religion*, ed. William A. Lessa and Evon Vogt, 234–43. New York: Harper and Row.

Turner, Victor. 1981. "Social Dramas and Stories about Them." *On Narrative*, ed. W. J. T. Mitchell, 137–64. Chicago: University of Chicago Press.

Urban, Greg. 1989. "The 'I' of Discourse in Shokleng." *Semiotics, Self and Society*, ed. Benjamin Lee and Greg Urban, 27–51. Berlin: Mouton de Gruyter.

Urban, Greg. 1996. *Metaphysical Community: The Interplay of the Senses and the Intellect*. Austin: University of Texas Press.

Urban, Greg. 2001. *Metaculture: How Culture Moves Through the World*. Minneapolis: University of Minnesota Press.

Walton, Travis. 1978. *The Walton Experience: The Incredible Account of One Man's Abduction by a UFO*. New York: Berkley.

Walton, Travis. 1997. *Fire in the Sky: The Walton Experience*. New York: Marlowe. On the Web: http://www.travis-walton.com/witness.html.

Welsome, Eileen. 1999. *The Plutonium Files: America's Secret Medical Experiments in the Cold War*. New York: Dial Press.

Williams, Raymond. *Marxism and Literature*. New York: Oxford University Press.

Žižek, Slavoj. 1989. *The Sublime Object of Ideology*. London: Verso.

# Index

*Abducted* (Clancy), 16
*Abduction* (Mack), 7
abductions and abduction narratives, 5–8; accounts of, 61–62, 64–68, 120, 143–46; and American Indians, 52–55, 58–60; development of national discourse, 113; deviations from standards in, 7, 113–14; government's complicity in, 51; hallmarks and facets of trope, 5–7; and hybrids, human-alien, 51; and hypnosis therapy, 6; and liminal sleep state, 15, 16, 124–25; of memories, 15, 65; and Native Americans, 165n3; and omniscience of abductors, 163n4; and organ harvesting, 51; origin story of the genre, 64–68; positive experiences with, 7; and pregnancy narratives, 114–16; and release narratives, 6; researchers' evaluations of, 7, 113–14; resistance to standards in, 117–18; signs of, 7, 76–77, 78; and sleep paralysis theory, 15–16; and spiritual growth, 8; support groups for (*see* Hillview UFO Experiencers Support Group); term, 6; transformative effect of, 7, 146; vocabulary of, 6. *See also* clinical procedures/experimentation; paralysis
accelerative culture, 158
Adler, Shelley, 163n8
aircraft, covert, 11, 81, 98
air space of residents, 92–94
aliens: and Area 51, 86–87, 141; autopsies of, 86–87, 166n1 (chap. 4); Cold War era perceptions of, 8; as colonizers/pioneers, 83; descrip-

tions of, 112; government collusion with, 51, 77, 83; and hybrids with humans, 51, 140–41, 144–45, 147; mind control powers of, 6, 55–58; in pop culture, 8–9; and reproductive organs/tissues, 57–58; Reptilian aliens, 76, 112; and Schwa stickers, 8, 163n7; technology (*see* technology of aliens). *See also* abductions and abduction narratives; captivity narratives
American Indians. *See* Native Americans
American West: genocide in, 43, 52, 55, 68, 101; as metonym for the past, 88–91; pioneer and UFO narratives of, 83; political struggles in, 103; and power of government, 102; and uncanny/ordinary interplay, 12, 80; value assigned to, 94. *See also* Native Americans
amnesia, 6
animals, cruelty to, 103–4
anthrax scares, 2
anti-corporate discourse, 107
antigovernment conspiracy theories, 2–3, 41–45, 75
anxiety, 2, 11
Apache-Sitgreaves National Forest, 61–62
apertures in the ordinary, 27
apophenia, 3–5; as channel into paranormal, 163n3; cultivation of, 26–27; and Hills' abduction, 67; narratives inspired by, 159; and power of uncanny stories, 18; resonance of, 19; in Stephanie's narrative, 30; UFOs as vehicles of, 24

appropriation, 10, 78

Area 51, 80–87; aliens held captive in, 51, 141; and autopsies of aliens, 86–87; and black (white) mailbox, 85, 87, 102; Cold War associations of, 11; and conspiracy theories, 80, 84; and disappearances, 141–42; employees of, 85; expansion of, 103; and hidden UFO, 81; highway closest to, 82; official acknowledgement of, 11, 98; *Popular Mechanics* story on, 100; Research Center, 103; residents' reactions to, 103; and revenue for local counties, 101; and reverse engineering, 80, 86; secrecy surrounding, 11; security of, 98–100, 104–6; and technology of aliens, 51; and tourists, 82, 85, 87, 101

Atomic Energy Commission, 11

atomic experiments, 62

*Aurora*, 11

autonomy of residents, 103, 104

autopsies of aliens, 86–87, 166n1 (chap. 4)

*Avatar* (2009), 78

Badmington, Neil, 8

Bakhtin, Mikhail, 24, 29

Barker, Bill, 163n7

Battaglia, Debbora, 18, 158, 166n2 (chap. 5)

Bauman, Richard, 24

Bell, Art, 44, 165n4

Berlant, Lauren, 2

Bible and biblical narratives, 128, 149–51

birther movement, 2

black (white) mailbox, 85, 87, 102

blind participants in UFO communities, 120

boarding schools of American Indian youth, 46–47, 50, 58–60

*Book of the Damned* (Fort), 163n3

Bourke, John G., 46, 48, 49–50, 76, 87

Branch Davidians, 12–14

branding livestock, 87–88

Canada, 129

canon of UFO lore, 111

captivity narratives: and abduction narratives, 113; and boarding schools of American Indian youth, 46–47, 50, 58–60; and clinical imagery, 61–62, 63–64; and colonization, 47; fantasy and factual accounts colluded in, 55; fictional forms conflated with, 53; as first American genre, 47; and freedom trope, 29; hallmarks of, 5–6; and Hussein, 62–63; and land seizures, 107; parallels between Indian captivity and alien abductions, 54–55; popularity of, 165n1; power reversals inherent in, 48; Puritan captivity narratives, 68–69, 71–72, 74, 165n7; the real of, 69–70; and release narratives, 29, 165n2; of Rowlandson, 165n1; and social memories, 52–55; and state as captor, 49–50; and transformation, 73; two-part tropes, 48; and vulnerable human body, 58; white captives of American Indians, 48–50, 53–54, 68–70, 71–75, 165n1; whites' American Indian captives, 48–49

Caruth, Cathy, 40

Castiglia, Christopher, 68

Catholics, charismatic, 38

cattle: cattle mutilations, 88–91; roaming on military property, 105

cave drawings of ancient Indians, 78

Central Intelligence Agency (CIA), 98

chains of semiotic association, 25–26

children, missing, 141–42

Christian discourses, 128–29, 149–51

civil liberties, erasure of, 2

Clancy, Susan, 16, 66–67
class issues, 42, 43
clinical procedures/experimentation, 62–64; and atomic experiments on humans/animals, 62; and cattle mutilations, 88–91; and pregnancy narratives, 114–16; and standard abduction narratives, 64; and Walton's abduction narrative, 61–62
Clinton, Hilary, 3
Clinton administration, 3
clouds and religious imagery, 128–29
*Coast to Coast* (radio show), 165n4
Cold War: and Area 51, 11; and human experimentation by the Soviet Union, 50; perceptions of aliens during, 8; surveillance technologies of, 81
collection centers, 45
colonization: by alien colonizers, 83; and captivity narratives, 47; and genocide, 43, 52, 55, 68; and Mather's UFO sighting, 70–71; and power relations between Indians and whites, 74; and UFO discourse, 76; white captives of Indians, 49, 50, 53–54, 68–70, 71–75, 165n1; whites' Indian captives, 48, 49
communicate, inability to, 55
*Communion* (Strieber), 5, 54–55
conspiracy theories and theorists, 41–45; and alien technology, 45; and Area 51, 80, 84; development of, 75; and environmentalism, 106; and government, 41–45, 92–94, 136–37; and Man-in-Black encounter, 162; and New World Order, 14, 106, 107, 136–37, 141; and surveillance, 157
containment, 6, 148
conversion trope, 137
corporate interests, 107
Corso, Philip, 86
cosmology, 77

*Crash at Corona* (Berliner and Friedman), 165n4
creativity, 159
Csordas, Thomas, 38
culture/cult overlap, 13, 14
Custer, George Armstrong, 59, 60

Dean, Jodi, 41, 163n1, 163n5
deaths, untimely, 30–32
Department of Motor Vehicles, 149, 152, 153–54
Derounian-Stodola, Kathryn Zabelle, 48, 165n3
desert tortoises, 103
disappearances, 141–42
disbelief in UFO encounters, 122–23
disempowerment, 79
disenfranchisement, 77
dissociative memory, 164n3
dog's black eyes, 24–25
Dog Star People, 77
Dorson, Richard, 70, 74
doubt, 126
Douglas, Mary, 159
Dreamland, 11, 80. *See also* Area 51

earth, poeticized, 127–28
Ebersole, Gary L., 165n1
eccentrics, 43
empirical descriptions of UFOs, 121–22
enslavement, 43, 78–79
environmentalism, 102, 106
Environmental Protection Agency (EPA), 102, 106, 107
evidence of UFOs, 84, 118–20
"Extraterrestrial Highway," 82
extraterrestrials. *See* aliens

fairy tale genre, 39
"fake invasion," 45
familiarity, sense of, 5
fantasy, 54, 55
Fassin, Didier, 40
fear, 110, 119, 125, 140–41
Feld, Steven, 17
*Fire in the Sky* (1993), 8

Indian Wars, 59
individuality, 137
industry around UFO information,
　51
injustices, historical, 157–58
*Intruders* (Hopkins), 113
Ivy, Marilyn, 166n4 (chap. 5)

Jacobs, David, 7
Jacobsen, Annie, 50, 166n1 (chap. 4)
Jakobson, Roman, 23, 158
Jemison, Mary, 165n2
Jones, Alex, 149
*Journal of Abnormal Psychology*,
　15

Kapchan, Deborah, 118
Kelly, Fanny, 71–73, 74
King Philips' War (1765), 49
Koresh, David, 12–14
Kripal, Jeffrey J., 163n3

land seizures in Nevada, 103, 106–8
language, poetic function of, 23
Las Vegas, 82, 152–53, 161
libertarian discourses and move-
　ments, 2–3
license, concept of, 148–49
licenses, driver's, 146–47, 148, 151,
　153–54
limbs, theft of, 21–22
liminality: definition of, 166n3
　(chap. 6); sleeping/waking state of,
　15, 16, 124–25; and uncanny nar-
　ratives, 159; and the weird, 118
Little A'Le'Inn: atmosphere of, 84–
　85; author's time at, 12; name of,
　82; owners of, 12, 81–83 (see also
　Travis, Joe; Travis, Pat); success
　of, 135; and tourists, 82–83, 84–
　85; *Weekly World News* coverage
　of, 140

Mack, John, 7–8, 163n5
magic, 39, 137
mainstream interest in UFOs, 9
Man-in-Black encounter, 161–62
marginality, 129–30

Masco, Joseph, 19, 41, 164n11
Mather, Cotton, 70
meaning: and conspiracy theories
　and theorists, 43; and repetition,
　23, 27–28; secret, 23
media: and Branch Davidians, 13;
　performance of power, 14
medical procedures/experimenta-
　tion, 61–62, 63–64; and atomic
　experiments on humans/animals,
　62; and cattle mutilations, 88–91;
　and pregnancy narratives, 114–16;
　and standard abduction narra-
　tives, 64
memories: abduction of, 65; alien
　control of, 6; of the author, 126;
　and continuity, 54; evoked by
　discourses of the weird, 126; false/
　screen memories, 65; fictional
　forms conflated with, 53; haunt-
　ing, 72; and hypnosis, 6, 65; and
　identity, 126; memory research,
　15; negotiations of, 64; ques-
　tioning *the real* of, 16–17, 73;
　recovered, 65; set-apart memory
　of Tom, 36–37; social memories,
　52–54
Menkin, Michael, 55–56, 58
mental illness, 20–22
Mexicans, 138
military: air space of residents,
　92–94; and crash site at Roswell,
　50–51; and land seizures, 106–7;
　power of, 94–95, 101–2; residents'
　reactions to, 97–98, 138; secrets
　of, 98; security of, 98–100, 104–6.
　*See also* Area 51
militia movements, 9–10, 14
mind control technology, 55–58
miners, 155–56
missing limbs, 20–22
mobility, 6, 131–35
modernity, 157, 160
MOVE bombing in Philadelphia
　(1986), 14
muse, 41
Mutual UFO Network (MUFON), 9,
　120, 121–22

narratives: and disbelief, 122–23; of Hillview Experiencers, 111–20, 122–24; of MUFON participants, 120–22; overlap in, 54; parallels between, 4, 19; and *the real*, 54; and speaking styles, 120–22; as theories, 18; as verbal art, 17

national identity, American, 7

nationalism, 137

Native Americans: and ancestry, 76, 78; artifacts of, 75, 108; and boarding schools, 46–47, 50, 58–60; cave drawings and petroglyphs of, 78, 97; and colonization, 52, 54, 83; idealization of, 75–76; and modern residents, 108; parallels between alien abductions and Indian captivity, 54–55, 165n3; and place-names, 66; and "power animals," 76; reservations, 103; of South America, 77; treatment of, in colonial era, 78; and UFO discourse, 75–76; and Walton's abduction narrative, 62; white captives of, 48–50, 53–54, 68–70, 71–75; as whites' captives, 48–49; and YouTube rap video, 58–60, 78

nature, crisis in, 127–28

Nazi-influenced imagery, 62

Nellis Air Force Bombing and Gunnery Range, 80

neoliberalism, 163n1

Nevada: air space of residents, 92–94; land seizures in, 103, 106–8

Nevada Test Site, 11, 51, 80

New Age discourses, 75, 78

New World Order: anticipation of, 136–37, 141; catalysts of, 14; EPA/BLM as tools of, 106; and land seizures, 107; and slavery, 136–37, 141

North American Free Trade Agreement (NAFTA), 138

nostalgia, 157

nuclear uncanny, 19, 41, 164n11

nuclear weapons, 50–51

numbers, repetition in, 27–28

occult and occult cosmology, 3, 12

omniscience, 24, 163n4

origin story of the genre, 64–68

Orr, Jackie, 11

overlaps in words, 14

ownership trope, 137

pacification of abductees, 7

parallels: and continuity in memory, 54; everyday life and uncanny, 97; identification and naming of, 157; in lives of experiencers, 33–34; between Native Americans and alien abduction stories, 54–55, 165n3; resonance associated with, 4; and signs, 151; as subject of uncanny stories, 19

paralysis: and American Indians/alien abduction parallels, 54–55; as hallmark of abduction narratives, 6; and repetition, 28–29; of Tom, 34–40; trauma associated with, 34–40, 164n3

Pearl, Daniel, 63

personal responsibility, 34

petroglyphs, 97

photographic evidence of UFOs, 84

pioneers and pioneer narratives: aliens as, 83; and iconic American past, 83, 87; modern iterations of, 91, 92, 95–97, 131; and Native Americans, 54; survival narratives of, 95; white captives of American Indians, 48–50, 53–54, 68–70, 71–75, 165n1; whites' American Indian captives, 48

Piper, Lenora, 74

place-names, 66–67, 166n2 (chap. 5)

planes: covert, 11, 81, 98; invisible, 101; small aircraft in Dreamland airspace, 99

Plato, 40

poetic function of language, 23

poetry, ancient condemnation of, 40–41

political ideologies, 9–10

popular culture, 8–9

Popular Mechanics, 100
posthumanist embrace of the other within, 8
postmodernity, 127, 163n7
power and *powers that be*: and American colonizing project, 54; and Area 51, 80; and autonomy of residents, 103; balance of, between Indians and whites, 74; and captivity narratives, 48; Carla's distancing from, 10; and class, 43; complex and contradictory views of, 94–95; and conspiracy theories and theorists, 41–45; and crash site at Roswell, 50–51; and freedom trope, 148; hidden power, 85; invisible centers of, 9; and license, 148–49; of military, 94–95, 101–2; omniscience of, 151; performance of, 14; political influence of, 3; and racial bias, 154; residents' reactions to, 102, 136–37; restrictive/possible effects of, 147–48; and technology of aliens, 51, 77; transformative effect of, 155
powerlessness, 35–40
pregnancy narratives, 114–16
Puritan captivity narratives, 68–69, 71–72, 74, 165n7

Rachel, Nevada: culture of, 11; *Popular Mechanics* story on, 100; proximity to Area 51, 10–11; and security at Area 51, 99; social categories of residents, 156; sonic booms in, 94–95; and tourists/tourism, 81–82, 101, 108; *Weekly World News* coverage of, 140; weird events around, 100. *See also* Little A'Le'Inn
racial issues and themes: and captivity narratives, 47; and hybridity theme, 65–66; and mixed-race couples, 65–67; racial bias, 153, 154
radiation experiments, 166n1 (chap. 4)

radio shows, late night, 44
*the real*, 15–18; and colonial captivity narratives, 68–69; and conspiracy theorists, 43; of memories, 16–17, 73; in the overlap of narratives, 54; reading the uncanny as, 22; in Tom's paralysis story, 36, 37, 39; and uncanny trama, 16; and the weird, 126; as what you *just know*, 43
Rechtman, Richard, 40
release narratives, 6, 29, 165n2
religious discourses, 128–29, 149–51
Reno, Janet, 10
repetition, 22–24; in numbers, 27–28; and paralysis, 28–29; and secret meanings, 23, 27–28; in Stephanie's narrative, 32–33; of traumatic memory, 40
reproductive organs and tissues: aliens' need for, 57–58; and development of abduction narratives, 5; and government complicity, 51; and pregnancy narratives, 114–16; and resistance to abduction standards, 117–18
Reptilian aliens, 76, 112
resonance of stories, 4–5, 22–24, 156–57, 159
restoration, 6
reverse engineering, 80, 86
roadkill, eating, 108–10
Robinson, Dennis, 67
Rockefeller family, 45
romanticization of the other, 78
Roper Poll, 7
Roswell, New Mexico: crash site near, 50–52, 75; and extraterrestrial bodies, 86–87; popular stories about, 165n4
Roswell International UFO Museum, 51–52
Roth, Christopher F., 65
Rothschild family, 45
Rowlandson, Mary, 49, 68–70, 71, 73, 165n1, 165n7
Ruby Ridge, 13, 14